More Prefaces to

SHAKESPEARE

By Harley Granville-Barker

EDITED BY EDWARD M. MOORE

A Midsummer Night's Dream
The Winter's Tale
Twelfth Night
Macbeth
From *Henry V* to *Hamlet*

PRINCETON, NEW JERSEY
PRINCETON UNIVERSITY PRESS

More Prefaces to

SHAKESPEARE

Contents

Preface

HARLEY GRANVILLE-BARKER'S *Prefaces to Shakespeare* have recieved wide acclaim since they began appearing in the 1920s. I think it is safe to say that Barker is generally recognised as one of the handful of twentieth-century scholars and critics who have made a permanent contribution to Shakespearean studies. Consequently, it seems well worth collecting all of his Shakespearean writings, some of which rank in importance with the best of the *Prefaces*, and include two of the full *Prefaces* never reprinted since their appearance in the original *Players' Shakespeare*. This volume contains the major pieces yet uncollected, and one essay, 'From *Henry V* to *Hamlet*', currently available in a paperback anthology (*Studies in Shakespeare*, ed. Peter Alexander, London, Oxford University Press, 1964), but important enough to be included here. I have added a brief introduction concerned primarily with Barker's work as a director, since that work is the source of his criticism.

The material was largely collected under a grant from the National Endowment for the Humanities and supplementary grants from Grinnell College, for which, needless to say, I am grateful. Acknowledgment is also due Professor Alfred Harbage, Emeritus, of Harvard, Miss Helen Willard and her staff at the Harvard Theatre Collection, and Miss Harriet Jameson and her staff at the rare book department of the University of Michigan Library. The bibliography compiled by Frederick May and Margery M. Morgan and printed in Purdom's biography, though not complete, has been an immense help.

Edward M. Moore,
Grinnell College,
Iowa

Introduction

HARLEY GRANVILLE BARKER[1] is remembered chiefly as an actor, playwright, director, and critic, but his major importance clearly lies in the latter two. As director, he not only established George Bernard Shaw as a dramatist, but he revolutionised Shakespeare in the theatre with three productions shortly before World War I. Indeed, W. Bridges Adams, in many ways Barker's disciple and successor as Shakespearean director, wrote later that if the war had not come Barker would not only have established a definite tradition of Shakespearean production, but perhaps have got the National Theatre he had been writing about for years.[2] After 1921 he did no more directing, although he did have an advisory role in five or six productions, one of them Shakespearean: Lewis Casson's *King Lear* at the Old Vic in 1940, with Sir John Gielgud in the title role.

From directing he turned to criticism, and most of his critical writing is on Shakespeare. He had written brief prefaces for the published acting editions of his three major productions (they are reprinted here), and in 1922 agreed to write prefaces for an elaborate, expensive edition of Shakespeare, *The Players' Shakespeare*, published by Ernest Benn Ltd. This edition, lavishly printed, reproduced the folio text, unaltered, and was illustrated by distinguished artists. Seven volumes were produced:

---

[1] He began using the hyphenated form of his name only after his second marriage in 1918. Most of the biographical information is from C. B. Purdom, *Harley Granville Barker: Man of the Theatre, Dramatist and Scholar*, London, 1955.

[2] 'The Lost Leader,' *The Listener*, July 30, 1953, p. 175.

Macbeth (1923), *Merchant of Venice* (1923), *Cymbeline* (1923), *Midsummer Night's Dream* (1924), *Love's Labour's Lost* (1924), *Julius Caesar* (1925), and *King Lear* (1927); Barker's prefaces were also reprinted separately. The venture was a failure and was abandoned. Barker continued writing prefaces, however, and revising ones he had already written; the collected *Prefaces to Shakespeare* are, of course, classics in Shakespearean criticism.

His critical writing comes directly out of his experience as a director. When Barker produced *The Winter's Tale* at the Savoy in 1912, elaborate, scenic Shakespeare was at its height. It was at the climax of a tradition begun when the theatres were re-opened in 1660, carried there by Sir Henry Irving at the Lyceum during the last quarter of the nineteenth century, and maintained by the fantastic productions of Sir Herbert Beerbohm Tree at His Majesty's. This was *the* tradition – in America as well – of Shakespearean production. There were a few voices against it, most notably G. B. Shaw when he was a London dramatic critic from 1894–1897, and William Poel whose amateur productions attempted to simulate Elizabethan productions. As already mentioned, Barker had worked extensively with Shaw; he had also worked with Poel: he played Richard II for him in 1899 and Edward II in Marlowe's play in 1903. But Barker's idea of producing Shakespeare was not Poel's.[3] He thought Poel's primary achievement was in demonstrating how Shakespeare's verse should be delivered. He wrote the *Daily Mail* in 1912 that Poel had demonstrated the ineffectiveness of the methods – especially the delivery of blank verse – of traditional Shakespearean production just as Gordon Craig – to whom Barker also acknowledges his indebtedness – had demonstrated the ineffectiveness of the 'illusion' of realistic scenery; in neither Poel nor Craig did he see a positive achievement.[4] In an interview with the *Evening News* shortly after his *Twelfth Night* opened, he said, 'At the Savoy we are trying to

---

[3] For more information on Poel see Robert Speaight's fine biography, *William Poel and the Elizabethan Revival*, Cambridge, Mass., 1954, or the present writer's 'William Poel,' *Shakespeare Quarterly*, XXIII, 1 Winter, 1972.

[4] Letter to the *Daily Mail*, Sept. 26, 1912.

establish a simple method of staging to create a simple shell into which you can put your ideas. I don't quite go so far as Mr Poel; I think his method is somewhat archaeological; there is somewhat too much of the Elizabethan letter, as contrasted with the Elizabethan spirit.'[5] The differences between the men were indeed great, but at the same time Barker was fully aware of how important Poel's work had been in breaking the tyranny of established methods of producing Shakespeare.

For Barker the necessity was, above all, to make Shakespeare 'alive' in the theatre, and it was to this problem that he devoted his attention. The primary question was not to discover how Shakespeare had been staged in Elizabethan times, but how he could be staged now without distorting the plays. To approach Shakespeare from any other angle, he felt, was to become involved in the 'accidentals' of Elizabethan stagecraft. If we should reconstruct an Elizabethan playhouse, have most of the audience stand in the pit, and use boys for the girls' parts,

> we should thus reproduce mainly the incidentals and accidentals, which the Elizabethans accepted without much question, but which – since we cannot convert ourselves into Elizabethans – we should find standing quite vexatiously between us and the *essentials* of the stagecraft.[6]

Of the essentials of Shakespeare's stagecraft, the poetry was foremost and demands the most attention. Barker saw much deeper into the essence of the poetry than did either Poel or Shaw, both of whom thought of the verse as an embellishment added to the drama itself. Barker saw that the very essence of the drama was poetry; he was of the opinon that 'great plays will always, I think, be found to be balanced constructions of character', but it is what follows from this that is more important:

> Shakespeare is intent upon showing us and upon emphasising not what they [his characters] do, but what they are. . . . Now if drama makes this demand only poetry can fulfil it. To consider

---

[5] *Evening News,* Dec. 3, 1912.

[6] 'Associating with Shakespeare,' London, 1932, pp. 16–17. The Presidential Address to the Shakespeare Association at King's College, London, Nov. 25, 1931.

verbal expression alone, we need some use of words of a more than rational power. Because with presentation of character involved, it is a question not merely of what a man thinks he knows about himself (or whatever part of that, rather, he may be willing to disclose; and a very partial and misleading revelation this would be!), but, added to this, and by far the more important, the things about himself he does *not* know.[7]

With the proper understanding of the function of the poetry, the rest of Shakespeare's stagecraft follows. He agrees with Shaw that scenery is a distraction since the poetry establishes an imaginative picture far more intense than all the resources of modern staging can produce, and because 'the picturesque environment to which modern staging has accustomed us' is foreign to his plays.[8] But the issue goes deeper than this; Barker points to the beginning of the last act of *The Merchant of Venice*, the lyrical dialogue between Lorenzo and Jessica. The effect of the dialogue is, indeed, to set a picture which the scene painters of the Lyceum could not rival,

> But even so, remark that [Shakespeare] is less concerned with the picture itself than with its emotional effect upon his characters, and . . . only through their emotions is the effect made upon yours.[9]

The picture in the mind's eye is of less importance than the characters before us, and this makes scenery irrelevant and an intrusion as well as distracting. Similarly, he points out that when Iachimo is in Imogen's bedchamber, as he writes down the description of the room he says only 'Such and such pictures; there the window, such The adornment of the bed', etc. because 'Shakespeare carefully refrains from calling attention to – something that is not there!'[10] But again the important point is that if the scenery were there it would only distract our attention from Iachimo, and in the scene with Posthumous when the contents of the room are described, the description is fresh for

---

[7] *On Poetry in Drama*, London, 1937, pp. 32–34.

[8] *Preface to* The Merchant of Venice (1930), *Prefaces to Shakespeare*, Illus. ed., London, 1963, IV, pp. 97–98.

[9] 'Shakespeare and Modern Stagecraft,' *Yale Review*, XV, 4, p. 716.

[10] *Preface to* Cymbeline (1930), *Prefaces*, II, p. 89.

the audience and gives extraordinary power to the maddening of Posthumous. A non-scenic stage is absolutely essential to the effect; it is impossible to gain the play's effect with scenery.

For his productions at the Savoy he approximated a platform stage by extending an apron out in front of the proscenium arch; this helped break up the picture frame stage, and gave an area close to the audience to help gain the intimacy of the audience, very much an essential of the Elizabethan stage.[11] The action was played forward as much as possible; several scenes were played entirely on the apron, cut off from the main stage by a curtain, and employing the side entrances to the apron. The opening scene of *The Winter's Tale,* for example, the dialogue between Camillo and Archidamus, was played on the apron before a blank curtain; at its conclusion the curtain rose on the palace of Leontes, the one scene moving immediately into the next. Curtains were used to block off the two areas of the stage for several other scenes as well.

There was no scenery: 'I would have none of it!' as he says in the preface to the acting edition of *The Winter's Tale.* There were permanent sets, decorative scenery as they came to be called. The two sets for *The Winter's Tale,* designed by Norman Wilkinson, were formal, even severe. The first, suggesting the palace of Leontes, was nothing but white walls and severe white pillars backed by gold curtains. For the sheep-shearing scene in the fourth act there was a backdrop of a simple cottage – very simple with harsh lines. There was direct lighting only; no footlights, no playing with shadows as even

---

[11] Richard Southern has effectively argued that extending the apron is quite a different thing from an Elizabethan stage (*The Open Stage,* London, [1952]). But Barker thought it was enough. In *Drama* (Publication of the British Drama League), N.S. 43 (December, 1924), p. 246, in reply to the London Shakespeare League's insistence on a platform stage for the proposed National Theatre, he wrote:

Personally I think that by using the apron stage and by contriving inner stage, balcony and doors as little within the lofty proscenium as possible, all the *essentials* of the Elizabethan theatre are preserved. And I would not plead for more. By all means, if space can be found, let us have a replica of the Globe stage also. But I fear its advocates would find that its use did more for archaeology than living art. They have taught the modern producer of Shakespeare a great lesson. Are they wise to be doctrinaire in the application of it?

Poel had done. The idea was simplicity with suggestion: of a palace for the scenes with Leontes, of a cottage for the sheep-shearing.

The costumes by Albert Rutherston[12] were colourful and bizarre, even outlandish. There was something Renaissance-classical about them, something of a 'once upon a time' conception to correspond with the fairy-tale romance of the play's action. The action was continuous with one 15 minute interval at the end of act three. The delivery of the verse and the movement of the play were rapid: in three hours the entire text of the play was performed except for six lines cut for reasons of obscurity (such as Polixines' 'sneaping winds' which was thought to be unintelligible, as distinguished from something like Leontes' 'Affection? thy intention stabs the centre' which Barker considered 'an intentional obscurity' indicative of Leontes' state of mind, 'a quite legitimate dramatic effect.'[13]

The critical reception was unfavourable, the production lost and was taken off after six weeks, though a few matinées did continue for a short time afterwards. The main charge was that by having the verse delivered so rapidly Barker had taken all the poetry out of the play and forced the actors to 'gabble'. John Palmer later pointed out in the *Saturday Review*[14] that the same reviewers had become used to the rapid delivery by the time of *Twelfth Night* two months later, and that much of the verse, particularly passages of Leontes', is unintelligible if delivered slowly. The fact of the matter is that the better critics had no trouble understanding the verse, and that most reviewers and playgoers, brought up on Irving and Tree, had never heard Shakespeare spoken properly. Barker himself answered the charge shortly after the production closed, in the preface to the acting edition of *Twelfth Night* printed below. There were also complaints of the 'odd' costumes and sets and the lack of scenery. Desmond MacCarthy, in a whole-heartedly favourable review, claimed reviewers and playgoers, brought up on scenic

---

[12] At the time Rothenstein. He anglicised his name during World War I. The drawings are now in Theatre Collection, Houghton Library, Harvard University.

[13] 'On Cutting Shakespeare,' a letter to the *Nation*, Sept. 27, 1919, p. 767.

[14] Nov. 23, 1912.

Shakespeare, did not know how to talk about anything else, and magnified the costumes and sets out of all proportion to their place in the production.[15] Shaw's comment on the reception is perhaps the best: 'What they didn't like was Shakespear [*sic*]. It will take them ten years to acquire a taste for Shakespear's later plays and learn his language.'[16] Harcourt Williams and John Masefield were lavish in their praise.

The critical about-face when *Twelfth Night* opened two weeks after *The Winter's Tale* closed substantiates the integrity of what Barker was doing. As Palmer and others noted the principles of mounting the play and the delivery of the verse were the same. The sets were again simple and formal (Wilkinson did both sets and costumes). The permanent set, Olivia's garden, was a formal garden with white staircases right and left at the rear leading down to a cupola in the centre supported by columns of pink and gold; similiar columns were used for porches at the top of the staircases. Four steps below the cupola were black and white benches with gold seats. The description may sound flashy, but a colour picture on the cover of *Play Pictorial* (XXI, 126 [1912]) shows pastel colours of a soothing harmony. Two formal wooden yew trees – obviously wooden – painted a dark green flanked the centre cupola. The scenes in the Duke's palace were played on the apron before a curtain – by a happy invention it seems to me – of black and white motley design, the only property being a motley throne for Orsino. Sir Toby's scenes were played around a table on an inner stage hung with a rich tapestry; the inner stage was also used for the prison scene.

Again the action was continuous, with brief intervals after II, iii and IV, i, and the entire text performed with the exception of a few obscenities and contemporary jokes whose 'savour', Barker thought, could now be got (if at all) only by learned editors. Again several time-honoured interpretations were thrown overboard; he speaks of several of them in the preface to the acting edition printed below – such as having Sir

---

[15] *Eye Witness*, Oct. 3, 1912.
[16] In an interview with the *Observer*, quoted in the *Boston Transcript*, Oct. 5, 1912.

Toby a gentleman: Barker later wrote Sir John Gielgud that he was a man who 'disdains to be drunk on anything but vintage Burgundy.'[17] For Feste he had the inspiration of giving the role to a musical comedy player, Hayden Coffin. The critics, naturally, were split over these 'unusual' interpretations, but the praise for Henry Ainley's Malvolio was virtually unanimous. The tradition of Malvolio as a sympathetic hero was discarded; he was seen to be egoistic, very much a prig, and ridiculous; Ainley did, however, give him a measure of acquired dignity after his sufferings. *Twelfth Night* ran to 137 performances.

After a year of non-Shakespearean plays, Barker returned to the Savoy in February, 1914 for another Shakespeare. He had originally intended to do *Macbeth,* and preliminary plans for it had been drawn up, but this was postponed because Ainley was bound up in the 500-plus run of Bennett's *The Great Adventure* (also directed by Barker) throughout 1914. He decided to do *A Midsummer Night's Dream* before going on to the tragedies. The production was successful, running to 99 performances, and was taken to America (with a much different cast) in 1915, but was even more controversial than *The Winter's Tale.* Judgments varied from the *Daily Mail's* 'a Shakespeare nightmare' to the *Sunday Times'* 'a revelation'.[18] A great step forward was indicated, however, by the fact that most of the controversy took place on Barker's terms. There was much less whole-hearted rejection and misunderstanding of the principles behind the production. London had been taught something.

The production followed the same general lines as the preceding two, but was brighter and more startling. Norman Wilkinson again designed the sets and costumes, and the company was roughly the same. It should be remembered that from Charles Kean to Beerbohm Tree *A Midsummer Night's Dream* was traditionally an excuse for the most lavish pictorial effects of any producer; Barker's non-scenic production was consequently even more startling despite the fact that most reviewers were by this time familiar with non-scenic Shakespeare. There

---

[17] Quoted in Purdom, p. 263.
[18] *Ibid.,* p. 149.

was no attempt at realism. The apron was covered with grey canvas, the main stage with gold canvas. The opening set of the scene with Theseus consisted of white hangings with gold arabesques and a throne back centre with steps leading to it; for the final scene the palace set consisted of white steps and severe columns touched with black, with black, rose, and white walls behind them. The set for the woods consisted of painted, billowing curtains as background, with trees in blue and green against purple. For the scenes at Titania's bower there was a rough velvet mound of bright green and a gauze canopy over it. The attempt was to suggest a contrast between the severity of the palace scenes and the soft mistiness of the woods. There was, of course, no Mendelssohn; the music was English folk tunes arranged by Cecil Sharp, and the dances English folk dances. Puck was played by a man (a heresy at the time) and there was a conscious effort (surely well taken!) not to play Bottom and his crew as a bunch of buffoons.

The most controversial part of the production, however, was the fairies. Except for the four that wait on Bottom, they were not children; they wore bronze tights and their faces and hands were completely gilded; their costumes, over the tights, were simple, colourful, occasionally outlandish, and many fairies had long rope beards or tinselled, crinkly hair. They moved consistently like marionettes, the effect being that of other-worldly creatures – Barker later wrote that 'the fairies must not tread the earth solidly at all.'[19] On a few occasions Bottom sneezes in the presence of the fairies, whereupon they shake, and Mustardseed even falls down. The exception to the fairies was Puck, whom Barker saw as 'pure English folklore' as opposed to the more exotic fairies, and dressed in a scarlet cloak with a wig of forest berries.

The production startled London indeed, and one may well question some of the effects in it; but then, as Barker pointed out, London did startle easily. He always insisted that any kind of scenery, scenic decorations, or settings were wrong if they called attention to themselves at the expense of the text, and his gilded fairies certainly seem to have done so. The colour

---

[19] *On Dramatic Method,* London, 1931, p. 72.

pictures of them in the *Illustrated London News* (April 11, 1914) are very impressive and, let it be admitted, rather startling even at this date. But Desmond MacCarthy's review is again especially revealing and, though MacCarthy had serious reservations about the production, tends to justify Barker's endeavour. He explains that he did not like the fairies the first time he saw the production; but after seeing them for the second time, he found that

> the very characteristics which made them at first so outlandishly arresting now contribute to making them inconspicuous. They group themselves motionless about the stage, and the lovers move past and between them as casually as though they were stocks or stones. It is without effort we believe these quaintly gorgeous metallic creatures are invisible to human eyes.[20]

* * *

It is the virtues of his production that he brings to his critical writing, for more than any other critic, Barker never forgets that he is dealing with a play meant for the theatre, and he approaches it as a director. A detailed study could be made — there have been short ones, but nothing exhaustive that I know of — of the relation between criticism of Shakespeare and the stage treatment of his plays. To oversimplify, but not, I think, distort, the broad outline of such a study would go something like this: From the time of Dryden (or maybe even Jonson) until the nineteenth century, Shakespeare is read for his beauties — the natural genius encumbered by the faults of his age and his own lack of judgment and knowledge; in the theatre we have adaptations instead of his plays. The nineteenth century continues this 'approach' in a sense but with a change in focus — Shakespeare by flashes of lightning, but the major focus is on character; we end up with Bradley reading the plays almost as if they were Victorian novels. In the theatre we have great character acting and the plays cut around the central characters, or frequently, character. There are of course exceptions. The

---

[20] *New Statesman*, Feb. 21, 1914. MacCarthy's two reviews of this production are reprinted in *Theatre*, London, 1954.

great achievement of twentieth century criticism has been the attempt to get at the *whole* play – through imagery, design, theme, etc. To this Barker and his successors such as Bridges-Adams contributed greatly in staging the whole plays simply and excitingly – not by going back to Shakespeare anachronistically, not by bringing him up to date à la Jan Kott and others (the method that seems to have dominated productions for at least the last decade), but by trying to get at the whole play and the essentials of the play in a modern theatre. It seems to me significant that Barker is the only major figure in Shakespearean studies to have distinguished himself both in the theatre and in the study. That his approach is valuable is shown by the constant demand for the *Prefaces* and the publication of this volume.

Preface to
The Winter's Tale

THESE FEW PREFACES make no pretence to Shakespearean scholarship, as that is usually understood. They are only the elaborated notes of the producer, who must view the play, first and last, as in action and on the stage. But it is, after all, a normal way to view it.

The Winter's Tale belongs to the final period of Shakespeare's work; it is essentially a product of middle age; it is a tragi-comedy. The technique of it is mature, that of a man who knows he can do what he will, lets himself in for difficulties with apparent carelessness, and overcomes them at his ease. But if this is a masterpiece, one questions several essentials of its making. One may wonder first at the break in the interest made by the passing of sixteen years. To a comedy this would be deadening; for in comedy, no doubt, the closer the action the better. To a tragedy it might be fatal; for, once well started, a tragedy must not relax tension. But in a tragi-comedy, as this is, is it not just some such jar that is needed to break the play from the one mood to the other? One may wonder at ' Time, as Chorus.' But it must have pleased Shakespeare, I think, to use once more, with mature skill, a device of his prentice days. Masters of their art are apt to enjoy doing this. And it is contrived that Time, in the middle of the play, shall definitely strike that note of tolerant understanding, the keynote of the whole play. A lesser artist, writing so, might stray towards indifference or cynicism; Shakespeare can sustain the tone of it beautifully. The very artifice of the device, moreover, attunes us to the artifice of the story; saves us, at this dangerous juncture, when Hermione is apparently dead, Antigonus quite certainly eaten by the bear, from the true tragic mood. Moreover, 'Time, as Chorus,' is the simple way to bridge dramatically the sixteen years, and therefore the right one.

There is more than one touch in the first half of the play, designed, I believe, to keep the tragedy a little less than tragic. Leontes' jealousy is never, as is Othello's, a strength, even a seeming strength (though of that comparison more in a minute); it is even less than a spiritual — it is a nervous weakness, a mere hysteria. He, poor wretch, moreover, even at his most positive, even while he sits in dignity and talks of justice, is conscious of this. After the one outbreak of rage with her, he never looks Hermione in the face, not through her trial, never until she has swooned. The man is a very drunkard of passion. Only in a passion of anger or cruelty, cold or hot, can he be sure of himself at all. Let him relax, and he is, as he says, a feather for each wind that blows. And the scene, coming nearest to true tragedy, where the babe is condemned to exposure, is yet heavily salted with the comedy of Paulina and Antigonus. At its height it becomes a slanging match. Was ever a character better contrived to keep the tragi-comic balance than Paulina? Little dignity is left to Leontes; and when any is restored to the scene, it is to Antigonus it falls as he takes the child in his arms to depart. Even in the scene of the trial when the tyrant breaks down under the sudden swift punishment of his folly, there is something a little ridiculous in his breathless confession to the surrounding courtiers, his frantic promises to undo what he has done. Paulina, too, relaxes from her high-toned scolding to an almost motherly fussiness, and the scene ends in pathos not in tragedy. But is it not this slight touch of the ridiculous which keeps it very human, and holds our sympathy; while the very suddenness of the catastrophe leaves us, paradoxically enough, expectant of some happier solution? Hardened into the finality of tragedy, the whole business would simply be too odious.

I believe there were three chief opportunities that Shakespeare saw in the old story of Dorastus and Fawnia. The first was this character of Leontes. Not so long before he had written

Othello. Othello is popularly supposed now to be a study of jealousy, and probably was so thought and spoken of then. But as Dostoievsky points out (or rather points out that Pushkin points it out; but I have never read Pushkin) this is not so.[1] It is the study of a primitive and noble nature, building its happiness upon a civilised ideal, and of the catastrophe that follows destruction of that ideal. Perhaps even Shakespeare himself had thought that jealousy was the centre-point of the *Othello* tragedy. It is a not uncommon thing for authors to set out with one scheme and complete another; he in particular was always building better than he knew when he began to build. Either way I imagine him seeing in Leontes a chance to retrieve that magnificent error, if error it was. If before he had set out to paint jealousy as a noble passion, and his own genius had defeated the false aim, now he would write a study of jealousy indeed, perverse, ignoble, pitiable.

Straightway he faced the first difficulty. Jealousy upon any foundation is less than jealousy, or more. Leontes has, as far as we can see, hardly the shadow of an excuse for his suspicion. Straightway he redeemed the blunder of Iago, that outrageous exhibition of theatrical virtuosity, redeemed it by writing this time no such character. That niche in the scheme is left vacant; and yet not vacant, but finely filled, for the wanton malice that is Iago the jealous man can only find, but finds surely, in his own heart.

The second opportunity in the play was, of course, the sheep-shearing scenes. Since the writing of *Henry IV*, Part II, he had not been able to bring English country life into the theatre to any purpose; not since *A Midsummer Night's Dream* had his simple rustics had their full fling. To Leontes' Sicilian Court enough foreign colour is conscientiously given in descriptions of Delphi, mention of the warlike Smalus, and the like; but Bohemia is pure Warwickshire, and there are signs that Autolycus was something of a portrait. 'He married a widow not

---

[1] *Brothers Karamazov*, Part III, Book viii, Chapter 3. Pushkin's remarks are in his posthumous *Table Talk, Sobranie sochineni,* Moscow, 1962, VII, p. 208. Pushkin's English title (as well as at least half the comments on Othello) derives from Coleridge's *Table Talk*, 2 vol., London, 1835, which Pushkin owned. Cf. Coleridge's remarks in the entry for 24 June 1827.

ten miles off, and compassed a motion of the Prodigal Son,' looks very like it. Though it is the merest fancy, I like to think of Shakespeare happening on that puppet-play at Stratford Fair, and on his Autolycus behind it. And if only Autolycus had brought it with him to the Bohemian sheep-shearing! Punch and Judy is the only motion left to compass nowadays, and that is dying. Has anyone ever the heart to pass one by?

The third chance, I think, that Shakespeare saw and seized was the last scene of all, with Hermione as a statue. The crude stage effect is so good that hasty naked handling might have spoiled it. Raw material at its richest is also the hardest to work in. But Shakespeare goes about the business with great care. He prepares the audience, through Paulina's steward, almost to the pitch of revelation, saving just so much surprise, and leaving so little, that when they see the statue they may think themselves more in doubt than they really are whether it is Hermione herself or no. He prepares Leontes, who feels that his wife's spirit might walk again; who is startled by the strange air of Hermione that the yet unknown Perdita breathes out; who, his egotism killed, has become simple of speech, simple-minded, receptive. The scene is elaborately held back by the preceding one, which though but preparation, actually equals it in length, and its poetry is heightened by such contrast with fantastic prose and fun. While from the moment the statue is disclosed, every device of changing colour and time, every minor contrast of voice and mood that can give the scene modelling and beauty of form, is brought into easy use. Then the final effect of the music, of the brisk stirring trumpet sentences in Paulina's speech, of the simplicity of Leontes' 'let it be an act lawful as eating.' Then the swift contrast of the alarmed and sceptical Polixenes and Camillo, then Paulina's happiness breaking almost into chatter. And then the perfect sufficiency of Hermione's eight lines (oh, how a lesser dramatist might have overdone it with Noble Forgiveness and what not!) – it all really is a wonderful bit of work. And, as the play is ending, I know few things that move me more than –

> I, an old turtle,
> Will wing me to some wither'd bough and there
> My mate, that's never to be found again,
> Lament till I am lost.

Plucky Paulina; such a good fellow! Her sudden betrothal to precise old Camillo may seem queer to us dramatic realists, but such symmetry was as natural to an Elizabethan dramatist as was the rhetorical final speech without which he would no more have ended his play than would a classical musician now finish a symphony without a full close.

One could draw out the parallel between *The Winter's Tale* and *Othello* by the very close comparison to be made between Hermione and Paulina, and Desdemona and Emilia. Paulina is certainly a better done figure than Emilia, and though interest is not centred throughout on Hermione (nor is it on Loentes, and for this reason only I think has the play been less popular with our leading actors), she is to me a most attractive and, for a 'good' woman, a remarkably interesting figure. 'Goodness' in drama is too apt to become a merely negative quality. But the poet-dramatist has the advantage of being able to clothe such characters in great verbal beauty. And beyond that in Hermione (and that is much) I seem to see an exquisitely sensitive woman, high-minded, witty too, and tactful. She had been under no illusions about Leontes, had questioned herself carefully before marrying him; since then had made his court a gracious, happy place, and to do that could have been no easy matter. One can tell that she knows the danger of the man, but when the outrageous blow has fallen, even in her utter helplessness, she has perfect courage. Against all the trouble facing her she stands serene; only the cruel side-blow of her son's death fells her. Even then she falls silently, proudly still. And Perdita! Though it may be only delightful girlishness as seen from middle-aged manhood, it is none the less delightful. No play of Shakespeare's boasts three such women as Hermione, Perdita, Paulina.

One notes the touched-in resemblances between mother and daughter, father and son. Polixenes and Florizel, light-hearted, impetuous, inconsiderate both. Perdita, with all her mother's courage and self-possession, which, at sixteen, is obstinacy too. And there are many other fascinatingly clever touches that go to make up the complexity of Leontes. There is a most daring piece of technique by which twice or three times an actual obscurity of words (their meaning could never have been plain to any immediate listener) is used to express the turmoil of his mind. Even the little scene of Cleomenes and Dion returning with the oracle is a model 'bridge' from the raucous revilings of Leontes over the helpless child to the dignity of the scene of the trial.

I make no contribution to the controversy over the division of the plays into acts and scenes. Whether they were first divided by Shakespeare himself or by a later hand I have no idea, though in some cases (not that of *The Winter's Tale*) the division is quite badly done. It is possible that the developing structure of the theatre and the stage gradually made the scene-division both an easier and a more important matter; and possibly in Shakespeare's own case, at least, the increasing length of the later plays necessitated pauses. But that any and every Elizabethan play, any drama of rhetoric and the platform stage, should be played as swiftly and uninterruptedly as possible – of that I have not the shadow of doubt. Therefore for *The Winter's Tale* I make the obvious and natural division into two parts, and allow for the one pause only.

How should the play be costumed? I was happy to find myself at one with Albert Rothenstein about this. Not in classic dress certainly. No matter for Apollo's oracle and Leontes, Tyrant of Sicily; it would offend against the very spirit of the play. But – just to give one's imagination the key – Renaissance-classic, that is, classic dress as Shakespeare saw it, would be the thing. And when we had quite made up our minds to this I suddenly thought and said to Rothenstein, 'Giulio Romano! There's our pattern designer recommended in the play itself.' It's little I know of Giulio Romano. Ought I to confess that Rothenstein could remember little more? But Giulio Romano was looked up, and there the costumes were much as we had forethought them. For the Bohemian countryside let us fetter ourselves as little as Shakespeare did.

As to scenery, as scenery is mostly understood – canvas,

realistically painted – I would have none of it. Decoration? – Yes. The difference is better seen than talked of, so I leave Norman Wilkinson's to be seen.

'Preface' to THE WINTER'S TALE: AN ACTING EDITION, London: William Heinemann, 1912, pp. iii–x.

Preface to
Twelfth Night

THIS PLAY is classed, as to the period of its writing, with *Much Ado About Nothing, As You Like It,* and *Henry V.* But however close in date, in spirit I am very sure it is far from them. I confess to liking those other three as little as any plays he ever wrote. I find them so stodgily good, even a little (dare one say it?) vulgar, the work of a successful man who is caring most for success. I can imagine the lovers of his work losing hope in the Shakespeare of that year or two. He was thirty-five and the first impulse of his art had spent itself. He was popular. There was welcome enough, we may be sure, for as many *Much Ado*'s and *As You Like It*'s and jingo history pageants as he'd choose to manufacture. It was a turning point and he might have remained a popular dramatist. But from some rebirth in him that mediocre satisfaction was foregone, and, to our profit at least, came *Hamlet, Macbeth, Lear,* and the rest. *Hamlet,* perhaps, was popular, though Burbage may have claimed a just share in making it so. But I doubt if the great heart of the public would beat any more constantly towards the rarer tragedies in that century and society than it will in this. To the average man or play-goer three hundred or indeed three thousand years are as a day. While we have Shakespeare's own comment even on that 'supporter to a state,' Polonius (true type of the official mind. And was he not indeed Lord Chamberlain?), that where art is concerned 'He's for a jig, or a tale of bawdry, or he sleeps.'

Twelfth Night is, to me, the last play of Shakespeare's golden age. I feel happy ease in the writing, and find much happy carelessness in the putting together. It is akin to the *Two Gentle-men of Verona* (compare Viola and Julia), it echoes a little to the same tune as the sweeter parts of the *Merchant of Venice,* and its comic spirit is the spirit of the Falstaff scenes of *Henry IV,* that are to my taste the truest comedy he wrote.

There is much to show that the play was designed for performance upon a bare platform stage without traverses or inner rooms or the like. It has the virtues of this method, swiftness and cleanness of writing and simple directness of arrangement even where the plot is least simple. It takes full advantage of the method's convenience. The scene changes constantly from anywhere suitable to anywhere else that is equally so. The time of the play's action is any time that suits the author as he goes along. Scenery is an inconvenience. I am pretty sure that Shakespeare's performance went through without a break. Certainly its conventional arrangement into five acts for the printing of the Folio is neither by Shakespeare's nor any other sensitive hand; it is shockingly bad. If one must have intervals (as the discomforts of most theatres demand), I think the play falls as easily into the three divisions I have marked as any. [Intervals after II, iii and IV, i.]

I believe the play was written with a special cast in mind. Who was Shakespeare's clown, a sweet-voiced singer and something much more than a comic actor? He wrote Feste for him, and later the Fool in *Lear.* At least, I can conceive no dramatist risking the writing of such parts unless he knew he had a man to play them. And why a diminutive Maria – Penthesilea, the youngest wren of nine – unless it was only that the actor of the part was to be such a very small boy? I have cudgelled my brains to discover why Maria, as Maria, should be tiny, and finding no reason have ignored the point.

I believe too (this is a commonplace of criticism) that the plan of the play was altered in the writing of it. Shakespeare sets out upon a passionate love romance, perseveres in this until (one detects the moment, it is that jolly midnight revel) Malvolio, Sir Toby and Sir Andrew completely capture him. Even then, perhaps, Maria's notable revenge on the affectioned ass is still to be kept within bounds. But two scenes later he begins to elaborate the new idea. The character of Fabian is added to take Feste's share of the rough practical joke and set him free for subtler wit. Then Shakespeare lets fling and works out the humorous business to his heart's content. That done, little enough space is left him if the play is to be over at the proper hour, and, it may be (if the play was being prepared for an occasion, the famous festivity in the Middle Temple Hall or another), there was little enough time to finish writing it in either. From any cause, we certainly have a scandalously ill-arranged and ill-written last scene, the despair of any stage manager. But one can discover, I believe, amid the chaos scraps of the play he first meant to write. Olivia suffers not so much by the midway change of plan, for it is about her house that the later action of the play proceeds, and she is on her author's hands. It is on Orsino, that interesting romantic, that the blow falls.

> Why should I not, had I the heart to do it,
> Like to the Egyptian thief at point of death,
> Kill what I love? — a savage jealousy
> That sometime savours nobly.

On that fine fury of his — shamefully reduced to those few lines — I believe the last part of the play was to have hung. It is too good a theme to have been meant to be so wasted. And the revelation of Olivia's marriage to his page (as he supposes), his reconciliation with her, and the more vital discovery that his comradely love for Viola is worth more to him after all than any high-sounding passion, is now all muddled up with the final rounding off of the comic relief. The character suffers severely. Orsino remains a finely interesting figure; he might have been a magnificent one. But there, it was Shakespeare's way to come out on the other side of his romance.

The most important aspect of the play must be viewed, to view it rightly, with Elizabethan eyes. Viola was played, and was meant to be played, by a boy. See what this involves. To that original audience the strain of make-believe in the matter ended just where for us it most begins, at Viola's entrance as a page. Shakespeare's audience saw Cesario without effort as

Orsino sees him; more importantly they saw him as Olivia sees him; indeed it was over Olivia they had most to make believe. One feels at once how this affects the sympathy and balance of the love scenes of the play. One sees how dramatically right is the delicate still grace of the dialogue between Orsino and Cesario, and how possible it makes the more outspoken passion of the scenes with Olivia. Give to Olivia, as we must do now, all the value of her sex, and to the supposed Cesario none of the value of his, we are naturally quite unmoved by the business. Olivia looks a fool. And it is the common practice for actresses of Viola to seize every chance of reminding the audience that they are girls dressed up, to impress on one moreover, by childish by-play as to legs and petticoats or the absence of them, that this is the play's supreme joke. Now Shakespeare has devised one most carefully placed soliloquy where we are to be forcibly reminded that Cesario is Viola; in it he has as carefully divided the comic from the serious side of the matter. That scene played, the Viola, who does not do her best, as far as the passages with Olivia are concerned, to make us believe, as Olivia believes, that she is a man, shows, to my mind, a lack of imagination and is guilty of dramatic bad manners, knocking, for the sake of a little laughter, the whole of the play's romantic plot on the head.

Let me explain briefly the interpretation I favour of four or five other points.

I do not think that Sir Toby is meant for nothing but a bestial sot. He is a gentleman by birth, or he would not be Olivia's uncle (or cousin, if that is the relationship). He has been, it would seem, a soldier. He is a drinker, and while idleness leads him to excess, the boredom of Olivia's drawing-room, where she sits solitary in her mourning, drives him to such jolly companions as he can find: Maria and Fabian and the Fool. He is a poor relation, and has been dear to Sir Andrew some two thousand strong or so (poor Sir Andrew), but as to that he might say he was but anticipating his commission as matrimonial agent. Now, dull though Olivia's house may be, it is free quarters. He is, it seems, in some danger of losing them, but if only by good luck he could see Sir Andrew installed there as master! Not perhaps all one could wish for in an uncle; but to found an interpretation of Sir Toby only upon a study of his unfortunate surname is, I think, for the actor to give us both less and more than Shakespeare meant.

I do not believe that Sir Andrew is meant for a cretinous idiot. His accomplishments may not quite stand to Sir Toby's boast of them; alas! the three or four languages, word for word without book, seem to end at 'Dieu vous garde, Monsieur.' But Sir Andrew, as he would be if he could – the scholar to no purpose, the fine fellow to no end, in short the perfect gentleman – is still the ideal of better men than he who yet can find nothing better to do. One can meet a score of Sir Andrews, in greater or less perfection, any day after a west-end London lunch, doing, what I believe is called, a slope down Bond.

Fabian, I think, is not a young man, for he hardly treats Sir Toby as his senior, he is the cautious one of the practical jokers, and he has the courage to speak out to Olivia at the end. He treats Sir Andrew with a certain respect. He is a family retainer of some sort; from his talk he has to do with horses and dogs.

Feste, I feel, is not a young man either. There runs through all he says and does that vein of irony by which we may so often mark one of life's self-acknowledged failures. We gather that in those days, for a man of parts without character and with more wit than sense, there was a kindly refuge from the world's struggle as an allowed fool. Nowadays we no longer put them in livery.

I believe Antonio to be an exact picture of an Elizabethan seaman-adventurer, and Orsino's view of him to be just such as a Spanish grandee would have taken of Drake. 'Notable pirate' and 'salt-water thief,' he calls him.

> A bawbling vessel was he captain of,
> For shallow draught and bulk unprizable;
> With which such scathful grapple did he make
> With the most noble bottom of our fleet,
> That very envy and the tongue of loss
> Cried fame and honour on him.

And Antonio is a passionate fellow as those west countrymen

were. I am always reminded of him by the story of Richard Grenville chewing a wineglass in his rage.[1]

The keynotes of the poetry of the play are that it is passionate and it is exquisite. It is life, I believe, as Shakespeare glimpsed it with the eye of his genius in that half-Italianised court of Elizabeth. Orsino, Olivia, Antonio, Sebastian, Viola are passionate all, and conscious of the worth of their passion in terms of beauty. To have one's full laugh at the play's comedy is no longer possible, even for an audience of Elizabethan experts. Though the humour that is set in character is humour still, so much of the salt of it, its play upon the time and place, can have no savour for us. Instead we have learned editors disputing over the existence and meaning of jokes at which the simplest soul was meant to laugh unthinkingly. I would cut out nothing else, but I think I am justified in cutting those pathetic survivals.

Finally, as to the speaking of the verse and prose. The prose is mostly simple and straightforward. True, he could no more resist a fine-sounding word than, as has been said, he could resist a pun. They abound, but if we have any taste for the flavour of a language he makes us delight in them equally. There is none of that difficult involuted decoration for its own sake in which he revelled in the later plays. The verse is still regular, still lyrical in its inspiration, and it should I think be spoken swiftly . . .

I think that all Elizabethan dramatic verse must be spoken swiftly, and nothing can make me think otherwise. My fellow workers acting in *The Winter's Tale* were accused by some people (only by some) of gabbling. I readily take that accusation on myself, and I deny it. Gabbling implies hasty speech,

---

[1] 1542–1591, naval commander, mortally wounded off Flores after holding off 15 Spanish ships for 15 hours. This exploit has been celebrated several times, notably by Grenville's cousin Sir Walter Raleigh ('A Report of the Truth of the Fight about the Isles of the Azores,' 1591) and by Tennyson ('The Revenge,' 1878). The wineglass chewing is told by the Dutchman Jan Huyghen van Linschoten in his *Discours of Voyages* . . . (London, 1598, a translation of the Dutch edition, Amsterdam, 1596). The extract concerning Grenville is reprinted in *English Reprints,* ed. Edward Arber, Vol. XIV, no. 29, pp. 90–96). There, however, the anecdote is given as a display of Grenville's being 'of so hard a complection'; Charles Kingsley's novel *Westward Ho!* (1855) relates that Grenville would chew wineglasses in a rage.

but our ideal was speed, nor was the speed universal, nor, but in a dozen well-defined passages, really so great. Unexpected it was, I don't doubt; and once exceed the legal limit, as well accuse you of seventy miles an hour as twenty-one. But I call in question the evidence of mere policemen-critics. I question a little their expertness of hearing, a little too their quickness of understanding Elizabethan English not at its easiest, just a little their lack of delight in anything that is not as they thought it always would be, and I suggest that it is more difficult than they think to look and listen and remember and appraise all in the same flash of time. But be all the short-comings on one side and that side ours, it is still no proof that the thing come short of is not the right thing. That is the important point to determine, and for much criticism that has been helpful in amending what we did and making clearer what we should strive towards – I tender thanks.

The Winter's Tale, as I see its writing, is complex, vivid, abundant in the variety of its mood and pace and colour, now disordered, now at rest, the product of a mind rapid, changing, and over-full. I believe its interpretation should express all that. *Twelfth Night* is quite other. Daily, as we rehearse together, I learn more what it is and should be; the working together of the theatre is a fine thing. But, as a man is asked to name his stroke at billiards, I will even now commit myself to this : its serious mood is passionate, its verse is lyrical, the speaking of it needs swiftness and fine tone; not rush, but rhythm, constant and compelling. And now I wait contentedly to be told that less rhythmic speaking of Shakespeare has never been heard.

'Preface' to TWELFTH NIGHT: AN ACTING EDITION,
London: William Heinemann, 1912, pp. iii–xi.

Preface to
A Midsummer Night's Dream

'SEPTEMBER 29th, 1662, . . . and then to the King's Theatre, where we saw *Midsummer Night's Dream*, which I had never seen before, nor shall ever again, for it is the most insipid, ridiculous play that ever I saw in my life. I saw I confess some good dancing and some handsome women, which was all my pleasure.' How many of us nowadays would dare confide that even to a cipher diary? But Pepys, as usual, is in the fashion. Shakespeare was out-moded, and the theatre manager was already bolstering up his mere poetry with sensuality and display. We have, of course, reformed all that. Still, if I must choose between this cheerful Philistine and the pious, awe-struck commentator, who tells me that 'The germs of a whole philosophy of life are latent in the wayward love scenes of *A Midsummer Night's Dream*,'[1] I turn rather to Pepys. He has done less to keep Shakespeare from his own. If you go to a theatre to scoff you may remain to enjoy yourself; if you go to pray (once in a while) you likelier leave to patronise.

Why waste time in proving that *A Midsummer Night's Dream* is a bad play, or proving otherwise, since to its deepest damnation one must add: Written by a man of a genius for the theatre, playwright in spite of himself? Does not vitality defeat doctrine? The opening of the play may be bad. The opening speech surely is even very bad dramatic verse. There is

---

[1] Georg Brandes, *William Shakespeare: A Critical Study,* tr. William Archer, Mary Morison, and Diana White, London, 1914, p. 71 (orig. pub. 1898).

nothing much in the character of Theseus; there's nothing at all in Hippolyta. The substance of the opening scene is out of keeping both with its own method and with the scope of the play. But before the end of it, earlier than usual even in his later days, Shakespeare has begun to get into his stride. If he couldn't yet develop character he could write poetry and –

> ... O happy fair!
> Your eyes are lode-stars; and your tongue's sweet air
> More tuneable than lark to shepherd's ear,
> When wheat is green, when hawthorn buds appear.

At the sound of that we cease to demand from Helena – for the moment at least – any more material qualities. How he could and seemingly couldn't help but flower into verse! It was still a question, I suppose, whether he remained a poet or became a dramatist. He was in every sense nearer to 'Venus and Adonis' than *Macbeth*. If he hadn't been a man of the people, if he hadn't had his living to earn, if he hadn't had more fun in him than the writing of lyric poetry will satisfy! If it was he made the English theatre, did not the theatre make him what he is – what he might be to us?

Next come the clowns. It is necessary, I am ashamed to say, to remark that Clown does not, first of all, mean a person who tries to be funny. A clown is a countryman. Now, your Cockney audience finds a countryman comic, and your Cockney writer to this day often makes him outrageously so. Shakespeare presumably knew something about countrymen, and he made the simple discovery and put it into practice for the first time in this play that, set down lovingly, your clown is better fun by far than mocked at; if indeed apart from an actor's grimaces he had then been funny at all. Later on Shakespeare did this, as he did most other things, better, but he never did it so simply. If Shallow and Silence are finer, they are different; moreover, though countrymen they are not clowns. If Dogberry is as good, he hasn't, for me, quite the charm. There are little sketches in the last plays; that delightful person, for instance, at the end of *Antony and Cleopatra* with his, 'I wish you joy of the worm.' But from the moment Bottom, gloweringly mistrustful of poor Snug, asks, 'Let me play the lion, too,' from that moment they have my heart, all five, for ever. It is a little puzzling to discover just how bad their play is meant to be. Did Quince write it? If he is guilty of 'Now am I dead,' then, is not the prologue a plagiarism? But a good deal of more respectable playwriting than this was plagiarism, as who knew better than Shakespeare? I suspect he was of two minds himself on the point, if of any at all.

Then come the fairies. Can even genius succeed in putting fairies on the stage? The pious commentators say not. This play and the sublimer parts of *King Lear* are freely quoted as impossible in the theatre. But, then, by some trick of reasoning they blame the theatre for it. I cannot follow that. If a play written for the stage cannot be put on the stage the playwright, it seems to me, has failed, be he who he may. Has Shakespeare failed or need the producer only pray for a little genius, too? The fairies are the producer's test. Let me confess that, though mainly love of the play, yet partly, too, a hope of passing that test has inspired the present production. Foolhardy one feels facing it. But if a method of staging can compass the difficulties of *A Midsummer Night's Dream*, surely its cause is won.

Lacking genius one considers first how not to do a thing. Not to try and *realise* these small folk who war with rere-mice for their leathern wings, that goes without saying. In this play I can visualise neither a beginning nor an end to realism of either scenery or action. Nor yet to use children. To my mind neither children nor animals fit with the theatre. Perfect in their natural beauty, they put our artifice to shame. In this case one is tempted, one yields a little, over Cobweb and Co. It's possible, even probable, that children served Shakespeare. But I expect that the little eyasses of that time were as smartly trained in speaking verse as is a crack cathedral choir now in the singing of anthems. That there might be a special beauty, an impersonal clarity, in a boy's Oberon or Titania I can well believe. To take a nearly parallel case, who would not choose to hear treble rather than soprano through Bach's *Matthew Passion*? This is an interesting point, and it opens up the whole question of the loss and gain to pure poetry on the stage by the coming of women players. But where are our children with the training in fine speech and movement? Stop beneath the windows of an elementary school and listen. Or worse, listen to the chatter of a smart society gathering; in the school playground at least there is lung power. It will take some generations of awakening to the value of song and dance, tune and rhythm, to re-establish a standard of beauty in the English language.

The theatre might help if it were allowed. Though, first of all, heaven knows, it needs to help itself. One may say that the tradition of verse-speaking on the English stage is almost dead. So much the better. Our latest inheritance of it, at the least, was unsound, dating not from Shakespearean times, the great age of verse, but from the 'heroic' days of Rowe and Otway; later from the translators of 'the immortal Kotzebue'[2] and the portentous Sheridan Knowles.[3] Comic verse found its grave (at times a charmingly bedizened grave) in the rhymed burlesques of Planché[4] and Byron. But Shakespeare was a classic and must be spoken 'classically,' and what you couldn't speak classically you had better cut. Look at the Shakespeare prompt books of even the last few years and see how mercilessly rhymed couplets were got rid of, blots upon the dignity of the play. From this sort of thing William Poel has been our saviour, and we owe him thanks. In the teeth of ridicule he insisted that for an actor to make himself like unto a human megaphone was to miss, for one thing, the whole merit of Elizabethan verse with its consonantal swiftness, its gradations sudden or slow into vowelled liquidity, its comic rushes and stops, with, above all, the peculiar beauty of its rhymes. We have had, of course, individual actors or speakers of taste and genius (one instances Forbes-Robertson), and there might be now and then a company inspired by such scholarly ideals as Benson could give, but Poel preached a gospel.

---

[2] German dramatist (1761–1819) immensely popular throughout Europe. Benjamin Thompson translated and adapted several of his plays for Drury Lane around the turn of the 18th century. Sheridan adapted *Die Spanier in Peru* as *Pizarro* in 1799.

[3] Popular English dramatist (1784–1862), a cousin of Sheridan and a friend of Hazlitt, Lamb, and Coleridge. He wrote many plays, including roles for Kean and Macready.

[4] English dramatist (1796–1880), extremely prolific, remembered mainly for his work with the Vestris-Mathews management at the Lyceum.

What else was Shakespeare's chief delight in this play but the screeds of word-music to be spoken by Oberon, Titania, and Puck? At every possible and impossible moment he is at it. For Puck's description of himself there may be need, but what excuse can we make for Titania's thirty-five lines about the dreadful weather except their sheer beauty? But what better excuse? Oberon is constantly guilty. So recklessly happy in writing such verse does Shakespeare grow that even the quarrel of the four lovers is stayed by a charming speech of Helena's thirty-seven lines long. It is true that at the end of it Hermia, her author allowing her to recollect the quarrel, says she is amazed at these passionate words, but that the passage beginning 'We, Hermia, like two artificial gods' is meant by Shakespeare to be spoken otherwise than with a meticulous regard to its every beauty is hard to believe. And its every beauty will scarcely shine through throbbing passion. No, his heart was in these passages of verse, and so the heart of the play is in them. And the secret of the play – the refutation of all doctrinaire criticism of it – lies in the fact that though they may offend against every letter of dramatic law they fulfil the inmost spirit of it, inasmuch as they are dramatic in themselves. They are instinct with that excitement, that spontaneity, that sense of emotional overflow which is drama. They are as carefully constructed for effective speaking as a messenger's speech in a Greek drama. One passage in particular, Puck's 'My mistress with a monster is in love,' is both in idea and form, in its tension, climax, and rounding off, a true messenger's speech. Shakespeare, I say, was from the first a playwright in spite of himself. Even when he seems to sacrifice drama to poem he – instinctively or not – manages to make the poem itself more dramatic than the drama he sacrifices. And once he has found himself as a playwright very small mercy has he on verse for its own sake. He seems to write it as the fancy takes him, badly or well, broken or whole. Is there a single rule he will not break, lest his drama should for a moment suffer? Is there a supreme passage in the later plays but is supreme more in its dramatic emotion than its sheer poetry? Take for an extreme instance the line in *King Lear*, 'Never, never, never, never, never.' Can you defend it as poetry, any more than you can defend 'Oh,

Sophonisba, Sophonisba, oh!'?[5] As a moment of drama what could be more poignantly beautiful? Whence comes the tradition that a blank verse play is, merely by virtue of its verse, the top notch of dramatic achievement? Shakespeare's best work, seen alive in the theatre, gives, I maintain, no colour to it. Verse was his first love, his natural medium – the finest medium for the theatre in general of his day, I'll admit. But how far he was, in principle and practice, from those worthy disciples who have for these centuries and do indeed still attempt to drag us wearily up their strictly decasyllabic pathway to Parnassus, only a placing of their work and his side by side in the living theatre will show. It has all come, I suppose, from learned people elevating him to the study from the stage. Despite the theatre; it revenges itself. I digress.

The fairies cannot sound too beautiful. How should they look? One does one's best. But I realise that when there is perhaps no really right thing to do one is always tempted to do too much. One yields to the natural fun, of course, of making a thing look pretty in itself. They must be not too startling. But one wishes people weren't so easily startled. I won't have them dowdy. They mustn't warp your imagination – stepping too boldly between Shakespeare's spirit and yours. It is a difficult problem; we (Norman Wilkinson and I – he to do and I to carp) have done our best. One point is worth making. Oberon and Titania are romantic creations: sprung from Huron of Bordeaux, etc., say the commentators; come from the farthest steppe of India, says Shakespeare. But Puck is English folk-lore.

How should the fairies dance? Here I give up my part of apologist to Cecil Sharp. I only know they should have no truck with a strange technique brought from Italy in the eighteenth century. If there is an English way of dancing – and Sharp says there is – should not that be their way?

And what tunes should they sing to? English tunes. And on this point Sharp has much to say – more sometimes than I can

---

[5] From James Thompson's *Tragedy of Sophonisba* (1730), parodied by Fielding in *Tom Thumb*. The line was later changed to 'Oh, Sophonisba, I am wholly thine.' Johnson refers to the line in his life of Thompson in *Lives of the Poets.*

quite follow him in.[6] I have no doubt there is a lyric missing at the end of the play, and to set a tune to the rhythm of Oberon's spoken words seems absurd. If this most appropriate one we borrow from *Two Noble Kinsmen* is not Shakespeare's (Swinburne thought it was), I'm sorry. I'm sorry, anyway, if it's vandalism, but something has to be done.

Finally, I divide the play into three parts. I don't defend the division; it only happens to be a convenient one. I can't defend any division, and some day I really must ask a modern audience to sit through two hours and a half of Shakespeare without a break; the play would gain greatly. This is less absurd, that is all, than the Jonsonian five act division of the Folio, for which, of course, there is no authority.

'Preface' to
A MIDSUMMER NIGHT'S DREAM: AN ACTING EDITION,
London: William Heinemann, 1914, pp. iii–x.

---

[6] See the 1924 'Preface' to *A Midsummer Night's Dream,* printed below, p. 105 and note.

Introduction to
The Players' Shakespeare

Preface to
Macbeth

Preface to
A Midsummer Night's Dream (1924)

From Henry V *to* Hamlet

Introduction to
The Players' Shakespeare

IN this edition of Shakespeare it is intended to present the plays from the point of view of their performance upon the stage. In no case, however, is the complete plan of a production set out. There has not been, indeed, the collaboration necessary to this between preface-writer and designers. For a complete plan — whatever its advantages — must involve many technical details, the setting out of which would weary all but the closely initiate. Moreover, no such plan, if it has life in it, ever ends in production as it begins on paper. The designer must think of his scenes in terms of his theatre, and of his clothes with some regard to the actors who will wear them. And the producer who cannot collaborate with his actors — however little or much they may be aware of the process — has mistaken his vocation. He had better be a drill-sergeant. These designs, then, show rather a general intention. Some of them, it will be seen, need be but little affected in their carrying out by any circumstance. In some, if circumstances were master, only the intention might finally survive. But intention — honest craftsmanship being latent in all covenants of the sort — is, after all, what counts. And the prefaces themselves may best be thought of as the sort of addresses a producer might make to a company upon their first meeting to study the play. The record of that study itself, if one could be made, would far out-value them, for the drama is above all an art of collaboration. They, too, do but exhibit an intention, to be checked, developed and amended in the actual, the very vital process of staging the play.

It will perhaps clarify these intentions, these opinions, and the better expose them to criticism, if certain postulates – in themselves but opinions, no doubt – upon which they are based can first be made clear.

It seems to me indubitable that the plays should be performed as Shakespeare wrote them. To this contention there is lip-service enough nowadays. But it must be remembered that the difference between Nahum Tate's *Lear* or Garrick's happy ending to *Romeo and Juliet* and Mr John Doe's omission of, say, six scenes from *Antony and Cleopatra* is one of degree rather than of kind.

Close upon this follows the question whether any omissions whatever from the text can be justified. Here, personally, I disclaim pedantry. The problem is not an easy one. There is – to put it brutally – its pornographic aspect. Shakespeare was by no means above making an obscene joke. The manners of his time permitted this to a dramatist. The manners of ours do not. Now the dramatic value of a joke is measured by its effect on an audience. Moreover, a joke is intended to make a specific sort of effect on an audience. And if, where it was meant to provide a mere moment of amusement, it makes a thousand people feel uncomfortable and for the next five minutes rather self-conscious, its effect is falsified and spoiled. And a series of such jokes may disturb the balance and alter the apparent character of the whole play. What the seventeenth century found harmless the twentieth may, as naturally, find scabrous. That is one aspect of the matter, and those who would ignore it forget that the performance of a play is, among other things, an exercise in public manners and that the legitimate sensibilities of the audience demand no less consideration than does the conduct of the actors themselves.

But, no doubt, when this consideration extends – as it has done in my own time – to turning 'God' into 'Heaven,' to Othello calling Desdemona a 'wanton,' and to such deodorizing of *Measure for Measure* that it is hard to discover what all the fuss is about, one inclines to see but the other aspect, and to say sharply that if people cannot suit their taste to Shakespeare's they had better do without his plays altogether.

Better not play *Measure for Measure* if you cannot play it before an audience to whom Angelo and the Duke, Pompey and

Lucio, Isabella and Mistress Overdone are fellow-creatures all. Othello must call Desdemona a whore, and let those that do not like it leave the theatre; what have such queasy minds to do with the pity and terror of her murder and his death? And to make Beatrice so mealy-mouthed that she may not tell us how the devil is to meet her at the gates of hell 'like an old cuckhold with horns on his head' is to dress her in a crinoline, not a farthingale. But the suppression of a few such jokes as are not customarily quoted even in prefaces nowadays, will probably not leave a play essentially poorer.

One might add that by the inclusion of many of the jokes the average playgoer will be made neither merrier nor wiser; for they are often quite hard to understand. And here the whole question widens. What is to be the fate of topical allusions whose meaning is lost? It would seem as if they must be by now mere dead wood in the living tree of the dialogue, and better cut away. It is certain that Macbeth's porter's farmer and equivo-cator can never raise in us the appreciative chuckle with which the original audience must have greeted their mention; hence probably the bibulous antics with which the baffled but mis-guided low comedian is apt in the modern theatre to obscure the lines. Rosencrantz's reference to the 'aery of children' is meaningless except to the student. But the logic that may excise this last had better not extend to robbing us of

> Dead shepherd, now I find thy saw of might;
> Who ever lov'd that lov'd not at first sight?

We have all laughed at Malvolio's reflection that

> The lady of the Strachy married the yeoman of the wardrobe,

but not one of us could say what it means.

The blue pencil is a weapon with which few are to be trusted. Its use grows upon a man too rapidly and too danger-ously. It solves too many difficulties far too easily. From cutting a phrase that may offend and a line that will not be understood to excising a whole scene that seems superfluous – and that does undoubtedly inconvenience the scene-painter! – is an enticing and a fatal progression.

Here is my own confession of faith upon the matter. I cannot regard every word that Shakespeare is supposed to have written as sacrosanct. He was not a perfect playwright; there can be no such thing. Moreover, he did not aim at perfection; very wisely, since drama, bound to its human medium, is the least perfectable of the arts. He aimed at vitality, and achieved it intensely. To vitality, then, in the interpretation of his work I would sacrifice preciseness. On the other hand, the plays have been so maltreated, both in text and construction, and we still remain so ignorant of their stagecraft, that our present task with them is, I think, to discover, even at the cost of some pedantry, what this stagecraft was. It may be that we can improve upon the original methods of their representation, but obviously we cannot till we know what these were. We must learn this, moreover, not in terms of archaeology, but by experimenting upon the living body of the play. For this purpose precise knowledge of the structure and usages of Shakespeare's own theatre will be as useful as a philosophic study of Hamlet's character may be inspiring. Neither, however, can tell us so much about the play as a play as its performance can. And it is about *Hamlet* and *Othello* and *Macbeth* as Shakespeare meant them to be presented in his theatre, that we need first of all to know as much as can be known. To this end we must experiment with a play as he has left it us. It is risky to say, even of the smallest detail, 'This is not essential,' or 'Shakespeare would have cut that without a word.' In practice one does sometimes take the risk. But – amazing as the statement may appear – Shakespeare's case as a playwright has still to be fully proved, and the proving it must needs be a thorough process. His plays have had every sort of treatment. Actors have twisted them up into swagger shapes, scholars have rolled them flat, producers have immured them in scenery. They have survived it all, and to say so much is sometimes thought to be the greatest tribute we can pay them. But there is another and a needful tribute; the setting out to discover what, as plays, they essentially are.

I have been led into the ambit of a second question. What, then, will be, for us, the most illustrative method of their staging? Again; the problem, if we consider it in all its bearings, is not an easy one, and it may not be capable of any cut and dried solution. To one method we have grown familiar; the fitting of the plays to our modern theatre. This may be justifiable on the ground of convenience, but it is unwise to put in the further plea that Shakespeare's art transcends all the circumstances of its interpretation. Apart from abuses that this practice has given rise to – let its advocates swear never again to cut or transpose a single scene to meet the scene-painter's convenience! – it is demonstrable that the very advantages of the modern theatre make it a round hole into which the square peg of Shakespeare's plays will not fit. We abjure the rounding of the peg. Very well. There is a sense, of course, in which a modern theatre must always be modern; but the question that remains is what can be done towards the squaring of the hole. Let us see first in what its roundness consists.

The equipment of the modern theatre has illusion for its main purpose; and, naturally, the better the equipment the greater part this will play in the theatre's proceedings. To the creation of illusion is added its power to stimulate emotion. Scene-painting and lighting are, in fact, set an important part of the task that in Shakespeare's time fell to the hands of playwright and actors alone. The structure of the stage has necessarily been changed to advantage illusion. And, with so much responsibility removed from them, the actors have been free to develop their art in new directions; generally to refine upon it. Whether, in general, this is to its loss or gain may be a question. It is arguable that acting, being so personal an art, stands only to lose by collaboration, and is best served by the dramatist who confides his play's every interest to its care. However this may be, it is clear that, collaboration once admitted, duplication of labour will tend to be eliminated and the whole art to develop along lines mutually advantageous to the collaborators. It might be added that if interests clash the least mechanical art will be apt to go to the wall. In an age, indeed, that still delights in machinery as in a new toy, scenic contrivance has often tended to make acting a nullity. But – such abuses of the partnership allowed for – since scenery found a place in the theatre, the art of acting has quite inevitably changed its tactics. It has accepted this new world of optical illusion which has been gradually created by the evolution of lighting and scenery, turned it to advantage and tried to forget, though not without some itchings of rebellion, its ancient freedom, its supreme dominance.

In modern times it is perhaps the dramatist who has been aptest to take advantage of the new state of things, and he at least has not been such an enemy to the actor as the scene-machinist has; though there are actors who will accuse him roundly. But – to come to grips with our difficulty – could we confront Burbage or Alleyn with *The Wild Duck* and *The Cherry Orchard,* what would they say? Would they appreciate the opportunity these plays give the actor to create the very illusion of life, their freedom from the rhetorical exposition of what may be delicately expressed by a sigh or a silence, their leisurely development of plot, their as leisurely unfolding of character, all the significance that the focusing of the footlights can give to insignificant things? Or would Burbage, admiring it all, yet exclaim in the very accents of the 'grieved Moor' that as far as he was concerned his occupation was gone? Are we, at any rate, too dogmatic if, conversely, we assert that actors whose natural bent it is to take advantages of these qualities in a play, will need to readjust their art very considerably if they are to fulfil the demands of plays written, not only in ignorance of a theatre with such resources, but written, in effect, in very defiance of them? And, *a fortiori,* what can this scenic equipment do for drama whose virtue it was to be independent of it? One need not perhaps jump to the conclusion that it can do nothing at all. But the gifts of the Greeks must at least be cautiously taken.

Approaching the question from its other aspect, it should be possible – and it is necessary – to distinguish between the artisic essentials and the merely incidental features of the stage for which Shakespeare designed his plays. But here we must move with caution, too. The practised artist will turn every circumstance of his work to its advantage if he can. We may pretty safely suppose that it was nothing but a nuisance to Shakespeare to have spectators sitting on the stage. But we shall be wrong if we think that he did not allow for and profit by the generally intimate relations between actors and audience that the platform stage permitted. It was doubtless most disturbing when the groundlings were rained on, and only a fanatic would say that an open air theatre was necessary for the full enjoyment of the plays. But the fact that they were played in daylight is evident in a hundred turns of their writing; and in those that it is guessed were written for the private theatres and candlelight certain signs of the change can be seen. A small matter this last, it may be, but not therefore to be ignored.

But to note some of the true essentials and to suggest how – if at all – our modern stage can conform to them.

Shakespeare paints a play's setting – should he think that it needs one – in its text, and no scene-painter by his art must discount this artistry. Its importance differs greatly as between play and play, so does its method. We may find,

> This castle hath a pleasant seat; the air
> Nimbly and sweetly recommends itself
> Unto our gentle senses;

and the description of the martins' nesting in the eaves that follows; or

> The air bites shrewdly; it is very cold.
> It is a nipping and an eager air.
> What hour now?
>   I think it lacks of twelve.
> No, it is struck.

Now there is surely no need to insist that realistically painted nests beneath undeniable castle eaves will distract the curious mind of the spectator just for that very short minute at the scene's opening in which the words are to be spoken from the words themselves and the speaker of them. And that should not be. But any scenic effect, realistic or other, which will detract from the importance of the actors as they begin these scenes, which will challenge their dominance, which will – if we may so put it – set up a direct relation between the audience and the beauties of Inverness Castle or the cold of the night at Elsinore in place of the indirect relation through the channel of the feelings of Banquo and Duncan, Hamlet and Horatio, that Shakespeare has devised, must react harmfully on the scenes, the characters and the performance generally. Here, then, is one problem for the conscientious scene-painter. He must solve it as best he may.

In *A Midsummer Night's Dream*, in a lesser degree to *As You Like it,* the text is a mass of scene-painting, and the difficulty is proportionately increased. The scene-painter should note, too, that Shakespeare has solved the problem as his stage presented it to him in a rather subtle way. When it was a question of touching in a summer sunset or a winter night and passing on at once to enthralling matters, he was content barefacedly for a moment to call our attention to what – so to speak – was not there. But when half the purpose of the play is to lodge us in a wood near Athens or in the forest of Arden, he either prepares our imagination by painting something which we are shortly to fancy, as he lets Puck describe Titania's bower, or he has a character picture for us some experience just past, as the first Lord and Oliver describe the wounded deer and Orlando's danger. He is careful not to put his actors into a direct antagonism with their background. Here, then, the scene-designer may conceivably ease matters. But if going further means coming into any sort of competition with the actor – to whom has been given a task which is also an opportunity – if there is to be any discounting of poetry by painting, it can be nothing but a disservice to the play. And if this presents a dilemma, it is for the scene-designer, not the actor, to avoid it.

Shakespeare takes liberties with time and space; his theatre allowed him to. Elizabethan playgoers let a night pass in three minutes and thought nothing of it. If they stopped to ask themselves where such and such a character, under their eyes at the minute, was supposed to be, 'On the stage' might well have served for an immediate answer. The stricter conventions of our illusionary theatre must not be allowed to curtail these liberties. This is a problem that every producer and designer of scenes must face. The refusal to face it makes havoc with such a play as *King Lear* and has all but banished that masterpiece, *Antony and Cleopatra,* from our stage.

There is one matter in which the plays themselves do not, either by text or construction, give us any consistent guidance, the matter of act and scene division. The Quartos, with one exception, boast none. The editors of the Folio set out to be clasically correct and to divide each play into five acts. In every case we find for a beginning

Actus Primus, Scœna Prima.

But sometimes they get no further at all; sometimes they mark acts and scenes, sometimes the acts only; once, in *Hamlet,* they give up the job half way through. I am not scholar enough to determine the significance of this. But, taken together, the attempt at uniformity and the failure to achieve it do not smack of Shakespearean authenticity. Moreover, what we know of the usage of the Elizabethan theatre goes to show that an act division might in practice mean one thing on one occasion and another on another; it might imply an interval for conversation and refreshment, or such a mere formal pause, filled, perhaps, with music, as we should now count a division between scenes.

Personally, I think it likely that Shakespeare's own practice in this matter changed, was never uniform; and, further, that it can sometimes – by no means always – be surmised from the purely dramatic construction of the play. Where it can be, and so has dramatic validity, it should, of course, be adhered to. But often it seems as likely that some other sort of convenience, connected with the structure of the theatre or the circumstances of the performance, was consulted. Altogether, it is a matter, I feel, in which the producer may be free to consult – not precisely his own convenience, but the dramatic interests of the play as he finally assesses them in relation to his own stage. He is by no means under any obligation of loyalty to the uncertain editors of the Folio, still less to their successors, who have not only followed this dubious path, but strewn it with more obstacles of their own devising in the shape of scene divisions and scene descriptions too.

The soliloquy was a vital part of Shakespeare's stagecraft. It was not merely a convenience for the disclosure of the plot. He used it as a means of bringing us into the closest contact with his characters' most secret thoughts and most passionate emotions. The physical proximity to the audience of the actor upon the apron stage, more importantly the absence of any barrier of light or of scenic illusion, bred a convention which fostered emotional intimacy. It was a case, as it often is with convention, of extremes meeting. As there was no illusion there was every illusion. Once grant that the man was Hamlet, the fact that you could touch him with your hand made him more actual to you, not less. And once admit that he thought aloud, you entered his thoughts the more easily if he moved in what was your own world still.

A producer of Shakespeare will find no more important and no more difficult task than the restoring of this intimacy of contact, without which the soliloquy must fail of its full emotional effect. A modern audience accepts the convention frigidly. Of modern actors it may be said that only the music-hall comedian is still quite at his ease in it, and even he tends to grow shamefaced and to wonder whether such goings-on are really 'artistic.' But if we want to measure Burbage's getting on terms with his audience when he began,

O, that this too too solid flesh would melt . . .

we should really recall (those of us that happily can) Dan Leno[1] as a washerwoman, or what not, confiding domestic troubles to a theatre-full of friends, taken unhindered to their hearts.

But convention is habit, and this lost one cannot be restored on demand. We know roughly the physical circumstances under which it flourished. How far their exact re-establishment is necessary is a question, and a matter perhaps for experiment. It is a further question how far this would suffice. Here, certainly, is a case for distinction between the essential and the incidental. For a first step one might set out to discover what most made for the actor's ease; for the rest the problem would be how best to coax a still unaccustomed audience into unconscious acquiescence in the expedient, whatever it might be. That these surpassingly emotional effects were obtained there can, I think, be no doubt. It has often been asked how such an unruly audience as we may suppose frequented the Globe Theatre had patience with the philosophical protractions of Hamlet. Does not this provide at least part of the answer? Certainly, Shake-

---

[1] 1860–1904, a very popular music-hall comedian.

speare never pinned so much of the fortunes of a play to a dramatic device of merely moderate value. The human ingredients of the problem have but superficially changed in three hundred years; we have only to order the others advantageously.

Then there is the question of costume. The Elizabethans were not what we should call logical on this point. They had a sense of strangeness, but no very definite sense of period. It is, indeed, only within recent times that antiquarian knowledge of this sort has spread, and even now one may suspect it to be rather falsely formalised in the average mind. We are apt to picture the clothing of the Greeks as colourless as their statues are left to us; we imagine Rome in the time of Marcus Aurelius inhabited by people wrapped in white togas; and most of us would be hard put to it to describe a street in our own London in A.D. 200. It may be that we do not know so very much more about the facts than Shakespeare did. Nor, it may be said, do the facts matter, for this purpose, except in the light of our knowledge of them. That might well have been the Elizabethan argument, and upon that basis we shall probably best face the difficulty.

At times Shakespeare's practice fits well enough with our own. In *Cymbeline* he means his Britons and Romans to be distinguishable at sight. In *Antony and Cleopatra* the picturesque difference between the rough soldierly Romans and the luxurious Egyptians is a calculated – and a well-calculated – effect. In *Macbeth* the Scottish lords wear some symbols at least of their nationality. But it is when we come upon Cleopatra saying, 'Cut my lace, Charmian,' that we have to pause and consider. And we have to remember our British Imogen in doublet and hose, and the conspirators paying their night visit to Brutus with their hats plucked about their ears. Now it may be argued that these things are trifles, anachronisms to which an audience pays no attention. That is a poor argument. The actors have to speak the lines. They cannot speak them with conviction if their appearance and action contradict the words, and the constant credibility of the actor should be a producer's first care.

But this is not the end of the difficulty. The plays, one and all, are full of references to Elizabethan customs. They are impregnated with what we may roughly call Renaissance feeling, some more, some less, but all to a degree. Of the recent history of his England Shakespeare had perhaps an historical sense comparable to our own. He certainly saw the Romans as great figures alien to him; though alien more in their moral outlook than in their daily habit. But the more vividly he imagined a character, the more it was his instinct to clothe it with familiar details. And if ever two men moved in the atmosphere of a sixteenth century court Hamlet and Claudius of Denmark are these men. If ever a scene in Shakespeare calls for the manners and bearing, the resources of attraction which we associate with the great ladies of Shakespeare's own times, it is the scene in which Cleopatra coquets with the departing Antony.

Now these are considerations that cannot be ignored. The very savour of the plays affected by them is concerned. But neither can one quite ignore our modern education on the subject. It may be a case for compromise. Sometimes the difficulty hardly exists in practice. To shift the date of Hamlet from A.D. 1000 to A.D. 1550 should trouble no one. If Cleopatra in a farthingale too dreadfully offends — well, a way out must be found. My own belief is that, submitting ourselves to the power of the play, that power being developed to the full by the cultivation of its every, of its tiniest resource, we shall have little trouble (after a first shock) in subduing our vision of it to all that was essential in Shakespeare's own. After all, we take Tintoretto's and Paolo Veronese's paintings of classic subjects with great calm.

To sum up: I have presumed in these prefaces upon the reader's general knowledge of what the Shakespearean stage was actually like. I assume that for a play's production nothing is to be designed or done that can obstruct or distort its action. And for a producer's motto I would suggest: Gain Shakespeare's effects by Shakespeare's means when you can. But gain Shakespeare's effects; it is your business to discern them.

If I am asked whether, with all the scene devising and designing in the world, we shall do better for Shakespeare than he did for himself upon his own plain stage, backed by a curtain and an inner room, surmounted by a balcony, I will answer that I doubt it, and do rather more than doubt. But nevertheless mere restoration of all this will not meet our case. We cannot quite discard the present, and, even could we, entering into the past would be a harder matter still. We should need to sit in an Elizabethan theatre as Elizabethans and be able as unconsciously, as spontaneously to enjoy the play. For spontaneity of enjoyment is the very life of the theatre and its art. This cannot be. Some half-way house of meeting must be found. But let it be insisted that the further we can learn to travel back upon the road the greater profit to us.

For instance, I assume (and tacitly, but for this remark) that no one would neglect to use Elizabethan music with the plays, and to use it just as Shakespeare did. The point does not seem to me to be even arguable.

Two matters I have left, and yet must not altogether leave, though they involve wider consideration, each in its kind, than can be given them here.

Shakespeare had no women on his stage. But for two hundred and fifty years and more we have been used to them, and it would not suit us to go back to a boy Juliet and to run the risk of a squeaking Cleopatra. Still, do not let us hastily assume that the change has been wholly a gain. There is as much to be said for a boy Rosalind and a boy Viola as there is for the banishing of women's voices from the singing of Bach's Matthew Passion; and for a boy Juliet and a boy Cleopatra much more. The methods of the Elizabethan theatre were never simply realistic, and the convention of the boy-actress is the most striking evidence of this. It went well with the other conventions of space and time, so appropriate to the platform stage; and especially it was fitted to the convention of verse. In this last lies the sheer beauty of the plays. And – frankly – this beauty ran a better chance of full and free expression through the medium of that pleasant artifice a boy's well-skilled interpretation could provide than charged with and coloured by the extremely personal attractions of such actresses as Shakespeare's stage would have found. Even now, though these social conditions have changed, the plays remaining as they were written for those original circumstances, it behoves the most devoted actress to remember that in the acting of these parts her sex is more a liability than an asset. Shakespeare, for instance, leaves no blank spaces to be filled in by that sympathetic suggestion which every modern dramatist allows for in scenes between men and women. He demands, on the contrary, a self-forgetful brilliance of execution which must leave prettiness and its lures at a loss, which indeed leaves sex and its cruder emotional values out of account altogether. How he would have written with women to write for it is idle to speculate. But it is plain to see how, having boys to consider, he set them no tasks which it was impossible or inappropriate for them to perform. Not that he fettered his imagination with respect to the characters themselves. Imogen and Beatrice, Constance and Cleopatra, are not the less women upon this account. But all art is selection, and Shakespeare's here lay in his choice of episodes and in his great skill in suggesting what he could not effectively present in direct terms. We have the passion of Constance over Arthur's death, we have no kindred scene for any mother with her baby in her arms. The wooing of Rosalind and Beatrice is a merry business; they set their wits and not their charms to work. Angelo's attack on Isabella is subtly intellectual. Othello's romantic wooing is over when the play begins; we see little but the tragic side of his relations to Desdemona. In *Romeo and Juliet* it is noticeable that the lovers are brought within actual touch of one another four times only, never for very long. The first time is at the ball, for twenty lines of fanciful conversing. The second is for the same space, and Friar Lawrence has them in hand. The third marks their tragic parting and the fourth their death. And in their great love scene -- one of the most beautifully passionate in all drama -- they are kept carefully apart.

Consider *Antony and Cleopatra*. Here one might suppose the very subject would force upon the dramatist scenes of sexual attraction. They are all avoided. When it comes to a description of her power over Antony, matters are not minced. But, as far as the play's action goes, she sways him by the moods of her mind, till the story takes its tragic plunge and mere sex is swamped in a greater passion.

Thus Shakespeare dealt, then, with this limitation that convention forced upon him. But did he not further positively turn it to account, transmute -- as all true artists in such cases do -- the offered poverty into wealth? He takes this chance to lift the relations of men and women to a plane where he can cope with them upon terms of poetry, or with a humour untroubled by those more primitive instinctive claims which they will make upon each other till that side of their love-affairs be settled. The stuff of tragedy and of the liveliest comedy lies without these narrow boundaries. And, working for a theatre forbidden such indulgence upon any terms that a sensitive artist could cope with, by mere circumstance Shakespeare found himself enfranchised. It is curious to reflect that not a little of the praise bestowed – mainly by women – upon the ideal womanliness of these heroines; their freedom, that is to say, from vulgarity, pettiness, coarseness, all their moral beauty, may be counted due to this circumstance that they were parts written to be played by boys.

This again leads me to the last point I must make. In the playing of Shakespeare one thing only is needful, or let us say that without this one thing all other virtues are vain. The plays must be spoken beautifully. Verse and prose were his sword and dagger. Let these rust or let them be ill-wielded, and no defensive armouring of a performance by scenery, costume, or even by well thought out acting will avail.

The speaking of Shakespeare is not a simple matter. He turns his verse to every sort of account, comic, tragic, pathetic, passionate, narrative, pictorial; he writes simply, he writes elaborately, at times he makes sound supersede mere sense, the music of the lines becomes their single power. But always, in this multitude of moods and methods, it seems as if it were a natural language to him. So it must seem to the actor and be made to seem to his hearers. Here lie more difficulties. Our ears are out of practice for such speech, even when tongues are trained to it. Many of the words are strange too, much of the syntax puzzling. Shakespeare's language has, in fact, to be learned before it can be rightly listened to, and playgoers must put themselves to that much trouble. Next, we must break the crust of false tradition beneath which the brightness and the vigour of this Elizabethan speech is hidden. For three centuries it would seem that our current talk has been flattening out and slowing down; and we make it ceremonious by pomposity. It is certain that Shakespeare's verse is meant to be spoken swiftly and yet with great variety of emphasis and tone,[2] that the voice must colour it richly and delicately, make such music of it as would appeal to a mind and ear to which the fine fretwork of Elizabethan music meant, as we know, so much. Each later generation seems to have dealt with it according to the taste of the time. Even as the plays themselves were deformed, so was the verse transformed by its speakers into strange shapes, till, in deliberate Victorian times, it bid fair to be flattened out and lose shape altogether. Here at least our newly cultivated historic sense should help us. If of every other art we have come to know that its virtues are the virtues of its time, why not of the art of the theatre as exemplified by its greatest master? We must re-train both our tongue to Shakespeare and our ears.

Even to train our eyes a little to the words as Shakespeare wrote them does not come amiss. It is to this end among others that the Folio text has been chosen for these books. For a first reading of the plays one would not recommend it, but the strangeness of it startles and makes keen again the too accustomed eye. The scarce interrupted lines seem to be written down as music; we are tempted to try speaking them aloud. This printing of the plays, with its modest nomenclature, scanty directions and ignoring of all scenic impedimenta – compare it with our modern elaborations! – does do much to give us Shakespeare as Shakespeare was. And this must be our starting-point if we are to go further and not fare very much worse indeed.

'Introduction' to THE PLAYERS' SHAKESPEARE, in
The Tragedie of Macbeth, London: Ernest Benn Ltd., 1923,
pp. ix–xxiv. (The first volume of *The Players' Shakespeare.*)

THE PLAYERS' SHAKESPEARE was begun in 1923, one play

---

[2] We have of course the best evidence that if this was not a general habit with the Elizabethans it was the particular quality that Shakespeare required of his actors. Though most Hamlets – not being playwrights – speak it calmly enough, there is some agony discernible in the famous speech. One doubts whether over the Town Crier treatment of his verse Shakespeare did not belie his famed gentleness a little. (Granville-Barker's note).

per volume, reprinting the Folio text, with illustrations by various people under the art-editorship of Arthur Rutherston, and with prefaces by Granville-Barker. Seven volumes (*Macbeth, Merchant of Venice, Cymbeline, Midsummer Night's Dream, Love's Labour's Lost, Julius Caesar, King Lear*) appeared before the series was dropped in 1927. Granville-Barker continued revising his 'Prefaces' and writing new ones until his death in 1945. This 'Introduction' was much revised for the *Prefaces: First Series* (London: Sidgwick and Jackson Ltd., 1927, and reprinted in all subsequent editions) so it seems useful to reprint the original version here. The 'Prefaces' to *Macbeth* and *Midsummer Night's Dream* following have never been reprinted.

Preface to
Macbeth

To pitch upon an informing epithet, *Macbeth* is the starkest of the great tragedies. It is the least discursive, even less so than *Othello*. With *Othello* it is the most forthright in its action; and this we should expect, for it is the tragedy of unchecked will, even as *Hamlet* is the tragedy of indecision. It is cold and harsh and unrelenting. If Shakespeare's mind was ever plagued by the doctrine of hell hereafter, this play might well be his comment on it. He puts hell here. Macbeth the man is a study in self-damnation. 'Hell is murky,' says the wretched woman in her sleep, and she may have further yet to go on to find it. But he ends as a soulless man, a beast, chained to a stake and slaughtered like a beast.

So much, if it be allowed, for general guidance in picturing the play.

The Text

We meet at once with an unusual difficulty. For long, producers of the plays have been mercilessly hacking at Shakespeare's authentic work, though the custom at last is losing credit. But in *Macbeth,* however conscientious we may be, there will be forced on us, apparently, work which is not his at all.

Hecate may be ruled out with hardly a second thought. If this be not true Middleton, it is at least true twaddle, and Shakespeare – though he had his lapses – was not in a twaddling mood when he wrote *Macbeth.*

The chief difficulty is with the play's opening. Good opinion holds that we do not meet Shakespeare's true text till Macbeth's own entrance with

> So foul and fair a day I have not seen.

If this be so, should the producer boldly begin here? It will make an interesting and very possible, and indeed a most dramatic, beginning. It will be in line with the forthrightness of the play's whole action. We should have this significant note struck at once by the protagonist; the weird sisters would suddenly and silently appear, as unexpectedly to us as to him, and the main theme would be opened with dignity and directness. The experiment might be well worth trying. But, almost certainly, this was not Shakespeare's beginning. Precedent is against it. The technique of *Richard II* and *Richard III* was far behind him; and, even though in the late-written *Antony and Cleopatra* there are but ten lines to be spoken before the chief characters appear, the difference between this and the speaking of the very first word of the play is, in theatrical effect, a great one.

On the other hand it is hardly more likely that he began with the witches.[1] Apart from such an opening being un-Shakespearean, the lines themselves are as little like Shakespeare as Hecate is, and have indeed all the tang of the Hecate lines. Critical glorification of the scene and its supposed purpose has not, of course, been wanting. But this mainly belongs to the class of commentary that deals with Norns and Shakespeare's knowledge of Northern mythology and the like, and need not trouble the simple theatrical mind, to whom a play must be first and even last a play. The scene – as better and sterner critical authority allows – is a poor scene and a pointless scene. And Shakespeare did not, at any rate, begin his plays with super-

---

[1] Incidentally it must be noted that in the text they are never referred to as witches, but always as the Weird Sisters. For witches the stage directions in the Folio are alone responsible. To these – with a text so extensively corrupted – it is difficult to assign consistent value. Where they pertain to the corrupted parts the balance of probability is that they are never Shakesperean. Otherwise they may be good evidence of the traditional staging of the play, but that will be the limit of their authority. The intrinsic evidence upon this question I deal with later. (Granville-Barker's note)

fluities. For all the offence to stage tradition, therefore, it may well be omitted.

Now comes the question of Scene ii. This, we may hazard, does at least stand for Shakespeare's beginning. That the lines themselves have been mauled is obvious, whether by Middleton, some stage manager, or the compositor. There is possibly matter missing. Even allowing for some desired effect of the confusion of battle and rebellion, the scene has not that expository clearness which is one of the hall-marks of true Shakespeare.[2] As Shakespeare wrote it, probably it was a better scene. But if, as we have it, it represents something of his intention, the safe plan is perhaps to take it as the play's beginning. It at least makes a fair start.

---

[2] The difficulty about the Thane of Cawdor can indeed be overcome by assuming that Macbeth is not 'Bellona's bridegroom.' Why must we suppose he is? For one thing, if the same battle is referred to, there would be little dramatic point in Duncan's question to Rosse,

> Whence cam'st thou, worthy thane?

and the answer

> From Fife, great king.

Certainly the duplication of 'Norweyan' is confusing. But are not these the facts? 'The merciless Macdonwald,' joined with a 'Norweyan lord,' was beaten by Macbeth and Banquo. Norway himself and the Thane of Cawdor were beaten by some other general. Even so it is strange that Angus should say questioningly of Cawdor,

> . . . Whether he was combin'd
> With those of Norway, or did line the rebel
> With hidden help and vantage, or that with both
> He labour'd in his country's wrack, I know not.

Shakespeare was not apt to leave things in such a muddle at the beginning of a play.

And all this does not, of course, exhaust the difficulties of the first four scenes as they appear in the Folio. The Macbeth-Duncan meeting is unsatisfactory. Moreover – and more importantly – the disclosure of Macbeth's mind, not in a soliloquy, but in two rather ineptly contrived asides, is surely, in such a play and with such a character, un-Shakespearean.

Even if – as some critics suppose – the explanation was that he hurriedly compressed an elaborately planned opening in order to arrive more swiftly at Duncan's murder, we should still expect to find the work more skilfully done. Here is a fantastic guess; but it might really be that when it came to printing the Folio the manuscript of the first four scenes – of Middleton's revision even – had vanished, and what we have is the result of the mobilising of memories of actors and prompter. Some lines they recalled accurately, some they confused, and some they had forgotten altogether. (Granville-Barker's note)

As to Scene iii Shakespeare may well have begun it with the weird sisters. But the present opening seems spurious, and it is quite out of key with the more authentic part of the scene. There is much to be said for boldly omitting it, and beginning, as aforesaid, with the entrance of Macbeth and Banquo.

This will dispose of the more serious textual difficulties. The porter's scene, both on the count of stagecraft[3] and on the aesthetic count, is surely genuine, and we have hardly sufficient cause to discard lines 37–59 of the scene between Lady Macduff and the child, though one must own to a suspicion of them.[4]

The entrance (Act IV, Scene iii) of the English doctor and the speech about the King's Evil is another matter. No doubt this is Shakespeare's work. It is equally obvious that he wrote it to please King James I, whom neither he nor we can any longer hope to please. But, upon kindred grounds, too much slashing may be done, and has been done. We must bring to the seeing of Shakespeare a certain historical sense. Besides, the episode has its dramatic value too. It helps to create – and there is little to do this – the benevolent atmosphere of the English court for a contrast with the description of Scotland in her agony. Certainly these twenty-two lines should be retained.

Staging and Directing

Upon a stage of typical Elizabethan equipment no difficulty of presentation need, of course, occur. And indications for the use of outer, inner and upper stage – though arguable occasionally – are not on the whole hard to follow. Until we reach

Enter Macbeth's wife alone with a letter,

the action is well enough suited to the outer stage. The weird sisters, at the Globe, *may* have appeared in the gallery. But Macbeth's 'Into the air' when they vanish, is no stronger evidence of this than is Banquo's 'The earth hath bubbles' that

---

[3] Macbeth must have time to get on his nightgown and wash his hands. (Granville-Barker's note)

[4] They show distinct signs of being an interpolation, but it does not follow they are Middleton's. Shakespeare himself might have found good reason for lengthening the scene in a wish to give greater importance to the two characters. See infra. (Granville-Barker's note)

they appeared on the ground. The dramatic effect, though, will surely be greater if they do actually stop the way upon that imaginary blasted heath.

Duncan's second scene could conceivably employ the inner stage; but then Lady Macbeth's first scene must be played above; and this seems, on the whole, an unlikely arrangement; — though a certain effect would then be gained by her descent later to welcome Duncan. But her first talk with Macbeth is an intimate one, and that argues rather the use of the inner stage.

Act I, Scene vii, might well be played on the outer stage; the procession of the

Sewer and divers servants with dishes and service

sufficing to mark passage of time and change of place. Still — the chamber where Duncan was supping being thought of as below — an effect could be gained by the drawing back of the inner stage curtains and the use by Macbeth and Lady Macbeth of the actual door of the inner stage as the chamber door. This would somewhat confine their scene together, perhaps to its advantage, and would also allow the lapse of time before Act II to be emphasised by the redrawing of the curtains.

Then for Act II the outer and — as I shall suggest — the upper stages will suffice. Macbeth's 'As I descended' is evidence that Duncan's sleeping chamber is imagined above. If we presume the curtains of an inner upper stage to be drawn close, there is no need for actual going up and down during the murder, and Lady Macbeth's quick re-entrance after her exit with the daggers would not be delayed. But it will be noticed that between Macduff's

I'll make so bold to call

and his re-entrance after the discovery twelve lines are spoken. This presumably leaves ample time for him to mount to the upper stage. Moreover, the effect of his re-entrance through the closed curtains and of his delivering,

O horror! horror! horror!

from the gallery will be very striking. The other characters would then assemble there, and there the rest of the scene would be played. One may suggest that what Shakespeare visualised was a number of people rushing out on the landing at the sound of the alarm bell, as they would in any country house to-day. They should be more or less in their night attire. This is connoted by

> And when we have our naked frailties hid;

and

> Let's briefly put on manly readiness
> And meet i' the hall together,

is fully pointed by situating the scene thus. It would be possible too – and effective – for Malcolm and Donalbain after

> Let's away; our tears are not yet brew'd,

to descend to the lower stage and finish the scene there. The last three speeches would then seem, as they should, a postscript to the rest, rather than an anti-climax.

Act III, Scene i, seems planned for the outer stage. Scene ii could be played there as well, but it might be more effective on the inner stage. The stage-manager's difficulty would lie in the setting of the banquet for Scene iv. But this should not trouble him. And unless there is to be a long pause before Act IV (and it should be noted that the scene between Lenox and another lord obviates any) he would have to be about as quick in clearing it away and setting the cauldron for the weird sisters. Scenes iii and vi are on the outer stage, of course. And for Scene iv the outer and inner stages are used together. Scene v is to be counted apocryphal.

The arrangement for Act IV is obvious; an inner scene and two outer scenes to follow.

In Act V the direct alternation of inner and outer scenes is arguably complete. But the stage directions for Scene vii suggest that, by the time of their insertion, at any rate, some more complex arrangement had been devised. Young Siward is slain, but there is no apparent provision for removing the body.[5]

---

[5] It cannot remain to the play's end. What is to hide it from Malcolm and Siward? (Granville-Barker's note)

There is also the direction for Macbeth and Macduff,

> *Exeunt fighting. Alarums.*

and immediately,

> *Enter fighting and Macbeth slain.*

Then, without a pause, and, again with no provision for the removal of the body,

> *Retreat, flourish. Enter with drum and colours Malcolm . . .*

And twenty-four lines later comes,

> *Enter Macduff with Macbeth's head.*

We may be fairly certain that the play is meant to end on the lower stage. If Macduff and Macbeth are to have a good fight, this – or at least the best part of it – should take place on the lower stage too. Now the double stage direction will be made clear if they can leave the lower stage fighting, and re-appear in the gallery.[6] If Macbeth is killed on the inner upper stage the drawing of its curtain would conceal his body. And if young Siward had been killed there too, there would be no pressing necessity for the removal of his. If then we may imagine, besides, the curtains of the inner lower stage drawn back and both outer and inner stages in use, the directions for the whole scene could read thus:

> *Alarums. Enter Macbeth above.*

MACBETH. They have tied me to a stake; I cannot fly . . .

> *Enter young Siward; either directly on the upper stage, or by crossing the lower stage from (say) the left door.*[7]

> *Alarums. Enter Macduff below by left door.*

MACDUFF. That way the noise is . . .

> *Exit by right door . . .*

---

[6] This would involve a momentarily empty stage, but the pause would be filled by alarums. It is a question, of course, how easily accessible the gallery at the Globe was from the lower stage. (Granville-Barker's note)

[7] Or the dialogue to the fight might even be spoken from the lower to the upper stage. (Granville-Barker's note)

Enter Malcolm and old Siward below by left door.

SIWARD. Enter, sir, the castle.

Exeunt through inner stage.

Alarum. Enter Macbeth below by right door.

MACBETH. Why should I play the Roman fool ...

Enter Macduff below by right door. ...

Exeunt fighting, either by right door, or, possibly, through inner stage. Alarums. Re-enter fighting on upper stage. Retreat. Flourish. Enter Malcolm, etc., in procession through inner stage.

This scheme would further suggest that Scene v might be played on the upper stage. The opening line

Hang out our banners on the outward walls,

gives some colour to the idea. But it is not a scene wholly of action. It contains the more or less reflective

To-morrow, and to-morrow, and to-morrow; [8]

and much would depend upon the immediacy of touch with the audience that such a position gave to the actor. That again would largely depend upon particularities of the theatre's construction. This is the sort of consideration that must often have ruled in or out the employment of the upper stage.

With regard to any scheme of staging other than the Elizabethan one can here but elaborate a little the general principles laid down already for a more liberal treatment of the plays. Presumably such a scheme would hang to some extent upon decorative effect. That it must never clog the action is axiomatic. As to the service it can render to this particular play; it can perhaps point the action by reinforcing the effect of swift movement through the earlier scenes of preparation and increasing tension to the murder of Duncan and its discovery. [9] It can perhaps do something to point the downward rush towards the

---

[8] But for the actor's treatment of this, see infra. (Granville-Barker's note)
[9] Though, actually, no swifter movement is well possible than that for which the Elizabethan stage provides. (Granville-Barker's note)

play's end, that counterbalances the opening rise in Macbeth's fortune. It can give us something of the barbaric grandeur with which we may suppose Macbeth would emphasise his regality. It can no doubt sharpen the contrast – though the play itself provides this by one stroke after another – between the court, the sights that the weird sisters show, the simplicity of Macduff's home, the kindly security of England and the unnatural strain of that scene of tragic twilight through which Lady Macbeth's tortured spirit drifts towards death.

It will be convenient to speak here of the act division of the play, for this is bound to affect the consideration of anything that can be called scenery. Elsewhere, in dealing with the plays generally, it has been suggested that we need not feel bound by the Folio's arbitrary division of each play into five acts, nor at any rate to the observance of an interval at the end of each. And there are some signs in this play at least that in practice this particular division was not originally observed.

The play, in the light of its story, falls into three parts. Acts I and II form the first and stand for the achievement of Macbeth's ambition. Act III, with the two first scenes of Act IV, form a second, which shows his wielding of power. From thence to the end we see the process of retribution. There are dramatic advantages in this arrangement.[10]

This first part is undeniably a unit of action; and in only one place does a halt seem to be called: at the end of Act I. Here a pause will have value, a pause, that is to say, which an audience can sit through in expectant silence. But a break in the tension, such as must be made by the usual inter-act disturbance and conversation, will be equally disastrous. What is wanted dramatically is, so to speak, a few moments' vacancy, in which the vibrations of the strenuous scene that ends with

> . . . I am settled and bend up
> Each corporal agent to this terrible feat.
> Away, and mock the time with fairest show;
> False face must hide what the false heart doth know.

---

[10] One need not spend time contending it was Shakespeare's. For is Shakespeare's discoverable? Upon what basis of dramatic advantage or practical convenience was it founded? (Granville-Barker's note)

may disperse, and the audience grow sensitive to the quiet opening of Banquo's

> How goes the night, boy?

If we are to imagine that the lights of the banqueting-chamber have been visible, or any snatches of music or talk heard coming from it, a slow darkening and silencing of these might gain the effect.

The second part, again, is a dramatic unit. And, if it seems to end with a comparatively unimportant scene,[11] it must be remembered that it is the murder of Lady Macduff and his son which precipitates Macduff's vengeance. This therefore leads us directly on to the third part.

It may be said that Act IV as it stands in the Folio is a better gathering of scenes. But there is this against it. Act IV, Scene iii (between Malcolm, Macduff and Rosse), is the hardest in the play to make interesting in its entirety, and it gets its best chance by being made an opening scene. Again, the sleep-walking scene, which, if Act IV of the Folio is left intact, must begin Act V, is at a grave disadvantage so placed, with its audience quite unkeyed to its necessarily subdued tone. On the other hand, the close connection of the two has great value. The contrast between Macduff and Malcolm's manly tune and the whisperings of the doctor and the waiting gentlewoman and the slumbery agitation that follows is well worth emphasising.

Let us come back to the question of the play's decoration. The barbaric splendour of Macbeth's court! That is the dangerous sort of phrase that slips into the mind when Shakespeare sets one's imagination free. The practical danger will lie, of course, in any attempt to capitalise this imagination in such extrinsic things as scenery and clothes, lights and music. We may make for safety by confining ourselves to such use of these things as Shakespeare himself had. If this appears an ignoble timidity, we must then at least see that they do not conflict with things intrinsic to the play. This principle will not be disputed

---

[11] The scene is most important, and has only come to be thought otherwise by the insistent viewing of the play as a dramatic preserve for the performances of Macbeth and Lady Macbeth. (Granville-Barker's note)

perhaps, but pitfalls in practice are many and unexpected. From some of the commonly less observed of them, however, *Macbeth* is freer than most of the plays.

The question of illusionary scenery need not be argued. Woe betide the painter upon canvas who will compete with

> This castle hath a pleasant seat; the air
> Nimbly and sweetly recommends itself
> Unto our gentle senses.
>   This guest of summer,
> The temple-haunting martlet, does approve
> By his lov'd mansionry that the heaven's breath
> Smells wooingly here; no jutty, frieze,
> Buttress, nor coign of vantage, but this bird
> Hath made his pendent bed and procreant cradle:
> Where they most breed and haunt, I have observ'd
> The air is delicate;

or with

> The west yet glimmers with some streaks of day:
> Now spurs the lated traveller apace,
> To gain the timely inn.

But if we are brought to ask, how did Shakespeare — the bare equipment of his theatre apart — visualise the setting of his play, there is evidence in the writing that his sense of period and place differed not so greatly from ours — if we are not too well informed in archaeology. He may, for instance, have passed blasted heaths between London and Stratford; and so, a very little further afield, may we. But is it the general colouring of the verse rather than any particular passages that seems to show Shakespeare's vision of a wilder country than his own; strange, yet not so strange to him that, for reasons of practical artistry, the difference was better ignored. Much of this verse-colouring no doubt concerns the characters more than their habitat. Even so, there is still an overplus for the broader effect.

That Shakespeare imagined — and that his actors wore — an unusual costume is shown by Malcolm's line upon Rosse's approach,

> My countryman; but yet I know him not.

Rosse may actually have worn nothing more symbolic of Scotland than a bonnet and a claymore, but the admission is enough.

Press too far on this path, though, and the pitfalls begin. Macbeth's castle, as we have seen, had the conveniences of the Globe Theatre; and the further suggestions of the night of the murder are rather of houses and habits familiar to that audience than of Scotland in the year A.D. 1000. Bells ring, people get on their nightgowns,[12] and the porter makes topical jokes. And though in the matter of costume we have neither Cleopatra's 'Cut my lace, Charmian,' to contend with, nor the subtler incongruities which crop out when we try to present the Italianate Claudius of Denmark as half a Viking, or Cloten, the player at bowls and provider of serenades, as an ancient Briton, in *Macbeth,* too, archaeology will insensibly undo us.

The decorator, then, of this particular tragedy may count himself lucky to be as untrammelled as he is, and so little plagued by such anachronisms (mostly of the modern mind's creating) as cripple an interpretation of the more strictly historical plays. Let him strike, may we suggest, an agreement with producer and actors upon the mood of the play, and help to project *that* into its environing and equipment; as, within these covers, Mr Charles Ricketts has now alone so admirably done.[13]

Music

Little enough use is, or well can be, made of music. There are few plays of Shakespeare in which this amenity – and all other such – is so sternly repressed. Hence, no doubt, Middleton's incursion with his songs and dances. It looks, however, as if the twice repeated inclusion of 'Ho-boyes' in the directions for Duncan's arrival at Inverness might be Shakespearean enough, and may indicate a festivity of welcome.[14] If so, it is just such a good stroke of irony as we should expect. The second direction may also indicate music during the banquet. It

---

[12] An Elizabethan nightgown, needless to say, was more a dressing-gown than a garment to sleep in. (Granville-Barker's note)

[13] The illustrator of the original volume.

[14] I do not know whether any archaeologically minded producer has yet substituted bagpipes. (Granville-Barker's note)

may; one can hardly say more. Here is a question of taste and matter for experiment. Certainly the horror of the scene for which Macbeth has left the chamber will be strengthened by a background of happy hospitality.[15] The contrast with the stillness to come and the fact that the scene which follows will call mainly for the same two actors in the same mood, should also be reckoned with. But it must be a distant background, no doubt.

Ho-boyes are noted again for the *Show of eight kings,* Banquo's descendants. And the recalling here by such unobtrusive means of Duncan's ceremonious welcome at Inverness would be valuable.

For Macbeth's kingship the Folio gives *A sennet sounded,* and no more.

But the drums, alarums, retreat and flourish of the battlefield must be considered. They are not meant to be mere noises. Just as the colours carried symbolised an army, so did these sounds symbolise upon that 'unrealistic' stage the varying phases of a battle. Treated as music they can be made symbolic; and though nowadays we have forgotten the alphabet of the convention, it is an easy one to re-learn. There is emotional value, too, in the sound of the trumpet. We need no learning to be stirred by that.

The Casting of the Parts

There will be the perennial difficulty of weighing the physical fitness or, it may be, the emotional power, of actors against their intellectual capacity. There can be no making of rules in the matter. To say that Macbeth must look like this or like that is to treat the play as a waxwork show. At the other extreme, to suppose that capacity to understand includes ability to express, is to confuse theatre with class-room. One may dogmatize a little upon temperament. One may – indeed one must – estimate the sheer, crude strength that a man needs to last out in the acting of such a part as Macbeth. One may sometimes say of any

---

15 If he can be thought of as breaking suddenly away from the jovial company, unable to play his hypocritical part in it any longer, a much needed impetus is given to the soliloquy. (Granville-Barker's note)

part or of any passage: This *cannot* be so. The rest is immediate judgment.

It is interesting to recall that the actress most identified in public memory with Lady Macbeth sinned most, and perforce, against her own notion of the part. Mrs Siddons says she thought of the woman as 'fair, feminine, nay, perhaps even fragile.'[16] But – in her famous years at least – she played her like an avenging goddess. Without doubt she builded worse than she knew; and – this is the pity of it – the tradition of her superhuman presence has misguided many a performance since. Let us set aside the fact that Shakespeare had a boy of seventeen to play for him instead of a woman of forty, 'massive and concrete' – to quote a classic criticism of quite another performance[17] – and see simply what demands the text makes. The first is surely for swiftness of method. Macbeth at the outset is the hanger-back, his wife is the speeder on. She is the gadfly stinging him to action. He will not 'catch the nearest way'; the night's great business must be put into her 'despatch.' Such small hints, though, are nothing beside the sweep of purpose that informs her every line in these scenes; and the actress who plays them slowly yields her prime function in the play's action.[18] And swiftness will imply lightness of touch, though neither, needless to say, must connote hurry. There is certainly no textual evidence that Lady Macbeth was physically fragile. For obvious reasons a dramatist does not crib, cabin and confine the realization of his work in such a way.[19] But the dramatic gain in making her so is hardly disputable. The effect of the 'undaunted spirit' is doubled if we marvel that so frail a body

[16] Mrs Siddon's comments on Lady Macbeth are found in Thomas Campbell, *Life of Mrs Siddons*, London and New York, 1934, chapter VIII.

[17] Herbert and Pip's compliment to 'Mr Waldengarver's' performance of Hamlet, *Great Expectations*, chapter XXXI.

[18] Incidentally the play's balance will probably at once be upset, for no actor of good instinct will allow a performance to hang fire, and if the Lady Macbeth will not set a pace the Macbeth will be tempted to, much to the prejudice of his own character's development. (Granville-Barker's note)

[19] Shakespeare hardly ever marks down the physical appearance of his characters. In Falstaff, of course, he does. But, in a sense, Falstaff's bulk *is* his character. Maria in *Twelfth Night* is 'the youngest wren of nine.' But the repeated insistence upon her diminutiveness seems to denote a particular player. (Granville-Barker's note)

can contain it. There will be an appropriate beauty in her faint-
ing. A small matter this; but Shakespeare himself has touched in
the incident so sparely that if it is not rightly done on the very
stroke there is no dialogue or extra circumstance by which an
error can be retrieved. And the thin-drawn tragedy of her end
will be deepened.

We should see her even physically weighed down with the
crown and robes that she struck for. When

> Our hostess keeps her state,

it should seem as if the lonely, wan figure upon the throne had
no strength left to move. She does make one amazing effort to
save Macbeth from himself and from discovery.

> Are you a man? . . . O proper stuff!
> This is the very painting of your fear. . .
> Fie, for shame! . . .
> Think of this, good peers, but as a thing of custom . . .
> I pray you speak not; he grows worse and worse.

This is the old fire upflaring. But it exhausts her. When the two
are left alone she can say no more, do no more.

> You lack the season of all natures, sleep.

What an emptiness of hope and help underlies the phrase! He,
at heart as hopeless, responds with the bravado of

> Come, we'll to sleep.

Later it will be made very clear what sort of seasoning sleep
brings to her. And when next we see her in slumbery agitation
we should hardly be sure, but for the concern of the doctor and
her gentlewoman, whether this wraith that sighs and mutters
and drifts away is still a living creature or no.[20]

Then there is the commonplace but important consideration
of the contrast with Macbeth. About him there must be something colossal; and if this primary effect cannot be obtained by

---

[20] By nothing I say do I mean to imply that such a thing as the acting
of fragility is impossible. But Mrs Siddons — for an instance — apparently
found herself at too great a physical disadvantage in the matter, and abandoned all attempt to suggest it. (Granville-Barker's note)

direct means, every indirect resource must be used to suggest
it. Not that mere physical bulk will avail. But Macbeth is a
valiant man and, even before he becomes king, of an almost
royal demeanour. He treats Duncan with a certain stiff dignity
and Banquo with condescension. Only his wife knows the weakness that his high manner hides. And when he is king this
demeanour is stamped even more deeply upon him. It has the
greater effect because he keeps alone. Does he do so because he
needs now to assert his will upon himself? Needs apart, he
appears to find some satisfaction in exercising it on others. The
length of the scene with Banquo's murderers has puzzled commentators. But is it not as if Macbeth, not content to give the
fellows their orders and their pay, wanted to subdue their wills?
One sees him pacing the floor and weaving words like spells
round the two wretches, stopping every now and then to eye
them hard and close. First he wants, above all, to commit them
to a deeper guilt towards Banquo. This shows later in his cry of

> Thou canst not say I did it.

Duncan might justly fill his dreams. But Banquo was their
enemy too, they hated him, they had done the deed: why then
should he be haunted?

From the time we first see him as king, the figure of the man
grows huger, harsher and gaunter. He loves his wife still. It is
partly his very love that makes him keep himself from her; why
should he damn her deeper with a share of the guilt to come?[21]
Partly, no doubt, it is that he knows she is broken and useless.
One of the few strokes of pathos that are let soften the grimness
of the tragedy is Lady Macbeth's wan effort to get near enough
to the tortured man to comfort him, But the royal robes, stiff on
their bodies – stiff as with caked blood – seem to keep them
apart. He has grown a stranger to her, who was once the

---

[21] Macbeth's views upon blood-guiltiness, however, were somewhat narrow,
if our interpretation (above) of
> Thou canst not say I did it

may hold. He would then expect his wife to be whole-heartedly glad, for his
sake, that Banquo was out of the way; it was enough for him to keep her
in a most formal sense innocent of the knowledge for her to be able to
applaud the deed with a clear conscience. (Granville-Barker's note)

inspiration of all he did![22] He treats her like a child:

> Be innocent of the knowledge, dearest chuck,
> Till thou applaud the deed.

Like an innocent child he cannot treat her. It is worth noting that, in this scene, Macbeth's mind is all upon the ill-powers of Nature – upon the powers that the weird sisters wield – as if it were their fellowship he now felt the need of.

We should mark, too, the bravery – and more than bravery – with which, later, he confronts the ghost. His nerves may give way, but he will not be the victim of his nerves. He dares it to come again, he drinks again to Banquo, his voice rises to the toast, clear, hearty, defiant. He means to test himself, to pit himself against every consequence of his deeds. 'Dare' is the note for all these passages. And, though he trembles still, it would seem that he wins; so to read,

> Hence, horrible shadow! Unreal mockery, hence!

and the ghost's vanishing.

Having outfaced this, he commits himself, from now on, to murder without scruple. And, as he loses humanity, he seems somehow to grow in physical strength. The power that went to make him man now goes to make him doubly brute, till, at the end, tied to a stake, he fights and dies like a wild beast indeed; and not till we see his severed head can we be sure that the evil life is out of him.

The actor of Macbeth has a mighty task. He must start at a pitch high enough to overtop his fellows; and the first part of the play will tax his judgment in balancing strength and weakness, conscience and ill ambition.[23] Between the

---

[22] To read

> But in them nature's copy's not eterne

as a suggestion of murder is quite wrong. From the point of view of the play's action a temptation to do what is already in the doing is weak. And this one line must then obscure the obvious meaning of every other line Lady Macbeth speaks in the scene. (Granville-Barker's note)

[23] For the foundations of Macbeth's character, and especially for a study of that power of conscienceless imagination that dominates it, one cannot do better than turn to the masterly *Shakespearean Tragedy* of A. C. Bradley. (Granville-Barker's note)

entrance as king and that line which looks to nethermost hell,

> We are yet but young in deed,

he has to carry his audience with him into such a world as Dante drew, where the spirit of man moves downward

> per l' aere amaro e sozzo.[24]

And in these scenes the technique of the play's writing, as it concerns the two chief characters, changes somewhat; and Shakespeare by his own great achievement adds to his interpreters' difficulties even while he offers them great chance of achievement too. For set the swift flow of the verse and the comparative directness and simplicity of the thoughts in the first part of the play beside this picture of the haunted desert of their souls, in which we are now to watch these two creatures moving, and note what a change of method is dictated to the actors for its realisation.

Macbeth's soliloquy in Act III, Scene i, and Lady Macbeth's four lines spoken alone in the following scene have clarity enough. But the rest of the dialogue is often but a mask behind which their minds are moving. Quite naturally, quite dramatically. Before they could talk freely to each other, these two. Now they cannot, and that in itself would begin their mutual tragedy. Sometimes the lines seem to carry echoes of a meaning which the speaker himself only dimly divines.

> It will have blood; they say blood will have blood;

and

> Strange things I have in head that will to hand,
> Which must be acted ere they may be scanned.

Here is more for the actor to do than to speak words, however expressively.

And, besides, there is all the unwritten motion of the play, the smiling menace to Banquo, the unspoken threat to the courtiers if they heed the 'strange inventions' that Malcolm and Donalbain are spreading abroad, the varied undercurrents dur-

---

[24] 'through foul and bitter air' (worse than that of Hell says the poet on the third terrace where anger is purged), *Purg.* XVI, 13.

ing the banquet scene. In all these attributes to the text the actor must, so to speak, clothe himself; yet, be it ever remembered that he must not *depreciate* the play's chief means of expression, the winged words and the verse that charges them with emotion.

From here to the play's end the part of Macbeth may be held to suffer somewhat from Shakespeare's plan of it inevitably lodging him in a dilemma. He means to brutalise the man, but a man so brutalised becomes less capable of poetic expression. The wild vigour with which the weird sisters are conjured comes naturally enough. But later, is not Shakespeare apt to leap this difficulty? Macbeth must moralise; so be it. But the sensibility of

> I have liv'd long enough,

and

> I 'gin to be aweary of the sun,

does not go over well in close conjunction with

> I'll fight till from my bones my flesh be hack'd.

It is not that the inconsistency could not be explained away. It is not even that there is in reality any inconsistency at all. It is rather that, within the narrow limits of drama at least, a character cannot be effectively developed in two directions at once. Shakespeare is hurrying Macbeth, defiant to the last, towards a hopeless doom. It is true that this quick shifting of mind in a man whose whole moral nature is in collapse, is a recognisable thing. But, with so little more to do to the character, Shakespeare has, for the sake of space perhaps, done some of it rather arbitrarily; and these passages – beautiful as they are, and, indeed, in their very beauty – are apt, straightforwardly interpreted, to seem to lie dead in the living body of the rest. Either so, or they require such subtle rendering as in itself is out of place.

When his wife is in question we do quite naturally catch the echo of Macbeth's earlier feelings for her, when he still could feel. The doctor tells him that she is

> . . . troubled with thick-coming fancies
> That keep her from her rest,

and his

> Cure her of that

comes, though hollowly, from his heart. But at once there follows the mocking

> Canst thou not minister to a mind diseased?

When he hears she is dead, by instinct he turns back silently to that earlier self to find his response. But there is none. He almost shrugs.

> She should have died hereafter.

Then, perhaps, he might have felt something, found some meaning in her loss. But now his only relief is to burst into a rage of pessimism. Whatever meaning has this life at all?

> It is a tale
> Told by an idiot, full of sound and fury,
> Signifying nothing.

It will be safe to suggest to most actors that in this last section of the play they should set themselves above all to avoid sententiousness. Macbeth sententious!

With regard to Banquo one can hardly do better than – with the thanks due for this as for so much else in the study of Shakespeare – quote Professor Bradley's analysis of his character.

'. . . Banquo is evidently a bold man, probably an ambitious one, and certainly has no lurking guilt in his ambition.'

'. . . he would repel the "cursed thoughts" [that the weird sisters had prompted in him]; and they are mere thoughts, not intentions. But still they are "thoughts," something more, probably, than mere recollections; and they bring with them an undefined sense of guilt. The poison has begun to work. [After the murder] . . . we may be pretty sure that he suspects the truth at once . . . He is profoundly shocked, full of indignation, and determined to play the part of a brave and honest man.

'But he plays no such part. When next we see him, on the last day of his life, we find that he has yielded to evil. The witches and his own ambition have conquered him. He alone of the lords knew of the prophecies, but he has said nothing of them. He has acquiesced in Macbeth's accession, and in the official theory that Duncan's sons had suborned the chamberlains to murder him. . . . He has, not formally but in effect, "cloven to" Macbeth's "consent"; he is knit to him by "a most indissoluble tie". . . . And his soliloquy tells us why:

> Thou hast it now : King, Cawdor, Glamis, all,
> As the weird women promised, and, I fear,
> Thou play'dst most foully for't : yet it was said
> It should not stand in thy posterity,
> But that myself should be the root and father
> Of many kings. If there come truth from them—
> As upon thee, Macbeth, their speeches shine –
> Why, by the verities on thee made good
> May they not be my oracles as well,
> And set me up in hope? But hush! no more.

This "hush! no more" is not the dismissal of "cursed thoughts": it only means that he hears the trumpets announcing the entrance of the King and Queen. His punishment comes swiftly, much more swiftly than Macbeth's, and saves him from any further fall.'

What better guidance could producer or actor ask?

The occasion of Macduff's introduction to the play should be noted. He appears in Duncan's train at Inverness, but does not speak. The discovery of the murder, however, is given to him. And it is obvious that Shakespeare requires a voice to ring out clear, candid and unafraid with

> O horror! horror! horror! Tongue nor heart
> Cannot conceive nor name thee!

His voice should be like light breaking in – even though it be a stormy sunrise. This extreme contrast with what has gone before is a very necessary effect. And candour is Macduff's keynote. He is placed in direct contrast to Macbeth; he stands, moreover, in blunt relief against the other tactful courtiers. Shakespeare is sparing of material in this play, but here is enough, and it can be given point to. The immediate

> Wherefore did you so?

when Macbeth lets out that he has killed the grooms, followed by observant silence, is worth, well acted and well arranged, a dozen expository speeches. By his retort to the pliant Rosse's

> Will you to Scone?
> No, cousin, I'll to Fife,

any sufficient actor can so fix the character and its dramatic purpose in our memory that his re-appearance even after many scenes will have full importance.

The scene in England needs as careful handling as any in the play and is commonly held not to repay the care; most producers hack at its text mercilessly. But this – principles apart – is penny-wise policy. The scene is the starting-point of the play's counter-action, and everything should be done to enhance its importance. Malcolm is to be king of Scotland. He is thought by most actors an ungrateful part, but Shakespeare at least did not leave him a nonentity. It will be useful to enquire why this scene is, as it is, a long level of verse, with its thoughts and emotions, till toward the end, rather catalogued than spontaneously springing. One simple explanation is that at this point in the play's writing Shakespeare was tired – as well he might be, after what had come before – but had to push on somehow. And we know that he all but transcribed a considerable passage from Holinshed. In the result the scene has been accounted dull – as dull, the irreverent might protest, as the virtue it chronicles. But we must look carefully to the playwright's intention. He needed for his audience, if not for himself, a breathing-space in which to recover from the shaking effects of the tragedy as he had so far developed it, and to prepare for the final rush of events. For this purpose a short scene would not suffice. He had already provided in the scene between Rosse, the old man and Macduff, and in the scene between Lenox and another lord, intervals of calm contrast with the bloody business of the play's main action. And it is, incidentally, most important to give these scenes their full value, to let the music of their smoother verse bring some relief to our ear, and the irony of their content – for the contrast is not a violent one – set our thoughts to work after our emotion has been so played upon.

But now neither would an unemotional scene suffice. Most certainly Scotland is not to be saved by the like of the cool time-serving Rosse and Lenox. They may be well-intentioned men enough. But Macduff marks even their greatest worth at such a time (and Malcolm's, as he thinks) with

> Great tyranny, lay thou thy basis sure,
> For goodness dares not check thee!

That Malcolm might be what his self-accusation would make him, that Macduff might be Macbeth's spy, that each then should turn from the other in loathing, and that Macduff should not be too easily convinced of the truth – all this is necessary as a solid foundation for the moral dominance of the rest of the play by these two. And the whole matter must be given space and weight to the measure of its importance. There is a formalism in the writing, true; and it may be more formal than Shakespeare could and would have made it at a more favourable moment. But even in the formalism there is significance. Malcolm is meant to be a young man who is deliberately virtuous, level-headed moreover, and astute. And however un-heroic such a figure may seem to the romantically-minded play-goer, Shakespeare will have it that this is the man to save Scotland. Given an actor of the right authority for Malcolm, the scene can be made interesting enough. A thing in it to make clear and stress carefully is the opposition between the natures of the two men and their ways of approach to each other: Macduff outspoken; Malcolm reserved, over-cautious at first, though never cold. From its beginning, indeed, the scene is, beneath the surface, well charged with emotion. And Macduff's line,

> Such welcome and unwelcome things at once
> 'Tis hard to reconcile,

which one has often heard an actor speak with an air of tame puzzlement, is really the passionate, half-choked utterance of a man still torn between hope and despair.

We have before noted the value of the little interlude of the doctor's entrance and the speech about the King's

Evil. And the rest of the scene is plain sailing.[25]

Rosse must be carefully cast. It is a 'stock-company' tradition that this part was the last insult that could be offered to a responsible actor. On the other hand pages have been written by an ingenious gentleman to demonstrate that he is the motive force and the real villain of the play.[26] To bring this home in performance, he would, one fears, have to be accompanied throughout by an explanatory chorus. But he is, in truth, a not uninteresting figure. The part is threaded more consecutively through the play than any other. Confronted with each catastrophe, Rosse stands emotionally untouched. He stands, indeed, as a kind of silent or smoothly speaking and cynical chorus to the tragic happenings. With great matter in hand, Shakespeare is, as we have noticed, thrifty in the writing of his minor parts; in this play thriftier perhaps than in any other. Unless, therefore, the producer so wills and most carefully contrives, nothing much can be made of the part. It is a negative figure. But that is its significance, and a most valuable one. And with care and intelligent acting this 'ever-gentle' gentleman, with his

> Alas, the day,

his

> Gentlemen, rise, his highness is not well,

his

> You must have patience, madam,

his admirable tact when he brings the news to Macduff of his children's and wife's slaughter, his smooth sympathy with Siward for his son's death, may be made very distinctive.[27] He

---

[25] May I register an opinion, though, that it is *Malcolm's* eye in Scotland that would create soldiers, and that it is Macbeth who is referred to as having no children. There is no proving this. But the implication that Macduff is there turning to Rosse for comfort is an unnatural one. (Granville-Barker's note)

[26] M. F. Libby, *Some New Notes on Macbeth,* Toronto, 1893 (cited in the revised *Variorum* edition, ed. H. H. Furness, Jr., Philadelphia, 1903.)

[27] He is silent at the discovery of Duncan's murder, and modern editions even omit to mark his entrance, which F1 gives with Macbeth and Lenox; but his silent presence can be made most effective. Or is the direction evidence of a mere stage-manager's anxiety to augment his crowd, and did Shakespeare's Rosse think it more politic to stay in bed when he heard the alarm bell? (Granville-Barker's note)

is more of a 'Renaissance' figure than the others. He is, in the old sense of the word, a politician. He is the play's taciturn *raisonneur*.

The part of Lady Macduff is in itself very easily effective; the child's part, mettlesomely played, even more so. The only trouble with the scene can be that it is too effective; within three or four minutes, that is to say, a direful catastrophe is precipitated upon two characters with whom we are hardly acquainted, and without, therefore, sufficient aesthetic cause. Shakespeare helps us over this difficulty by giving scope for a well-coloured, positive personality; and this should determine a Lady Macduff's casting. With her first line she can make herself sufficiently known to the audience:

What had he done to make him fly the land?

It is important, too, that the killing of the child should be done very deliberately. The thing is so abhorrent that we are apt to try and gloss it over in action. This is a mistake. The dramatic enormity is belittled by the open-eyed, heroic readiness with which the child faces death. This heroism strikes the note upon which the scene must end.

To pass upon some details. There is a tradition – one of those quite unreliable stage traditions – which speaks of the porter as the Drunken Porter, and makes him in appearance a candidate for an inebriates' home. For such a painful effort at comedy Shakespeare gives us no warrant. Truly the porter had been carousing till the second cock, and no doubt the news of the victory and the king's visit made it a good occasion for getting drunk. But he answers Macduff's joke about it quite aptly, and his delay in opening the gates can presumably be accounted for by his unwilling waking, the getting on of clothes and boots, and the finding a light for his lantern. Drunk on this occasion and on others he may have been, but it does not prove him a confirmed sot.

Banquo's murderers are commonly made ruffians fetched from the gutter. But the text's implication is surely that they were officers, cast perhaps for some misdemeanour and out of luck. Certainly the lovely lines,

> The west yet glimmers with some sreaks of day.
> Now spurs the lated traveller apace
> To gain the timely inn,

are not gutter-bred, and Macbeth's speech to them, beginning,

> Ay, in the catalogue ye go for men,

loses half its point if they are not men come down in the world.
The third murderer is obviously a private and particular spy of
Macbeth's, and his unheralded appearance (like that of the
fellow who warns Lady Macduff of her danger) is in itself
significant enough, significant too of the whole state of Macbeth's kingdom, with its spies, and spies upon spies; when, as
Rosse says,

> . . . we hold rumour
> From what we fear, yet know not what we fear.

We must note, too, the masterly effect produced when these
three stand with Banquo's body at their feet, the light out, and
the stillness around — which they but half break with their curt
whispering.

It is important that the doctor and the waiting gentlewoman
should not — as the stage phrase goes — try to play Lady
Macbeth's part for her in the sleep-walking scene. He is intent
on his case, she mainly obsessed with a queen's waiting-
woman's anxiety to hush up the scandal. Beside Lady Macbeth
herself they must seem pettifogging, or she cannot show tragic
to the full. The doctor has his couplet too, when Macbeth has
flung off the stage in berserk rage:

> Were I from Dunsinane away and clear,
> Profit again should hardly draw me here.

This has been condemned as un-Shakespearean and beneath the
dignity of the tragedy. But when Shakespeare saw a chance to
salt the meat of his plays with such touches he did not stand
upon tragic dignity. He had enough of that to spare and to
waste upon us whenever he chose.

Duncan can hardly be misread. He is often made older than
need be, and sometimes too consistently meek and usually too
lachrymose. There are actors with an unhappy knack of taking

one point in a part – and a minor one – as a peg upon which to hang the whole. And Duncan's 'plenteous joys' seeking to hide themselves in 'drops of sorrow' are apt to be used to water the character down to an undue depression; and with this will sag the play's whole beginning, one aspect of which the king's figure must dominate. His arrival at Inverness should be, in a simple way, as stately as possible. His lines here have fine turns of thought and feeling, and a most royal ring about them. And

> By your leave, hostess,

seems to indicate that, as the custom was, he kisses Lady Macbeth's cheek. What better climax and ending could the scene have?

The problem of presenting the weird sisters is more deeply rooted than in any corruption of the text. We can cut away most of Middleton with confidence, and quite banish his creatures of comic opera from our minds, and the remainder may be true Shakespeare; but what the positive embodiment of Shakespeare's conception should be this simple sum in subtraction by no means leaves clear. That he himself calls them weird sisters and not (proveably) witches is something, and might lead us straight to Holinshed's 'three women in strange and wild apparel, resembling creatures of elder world,' if it were not that both Holinshed in another passage and Shakespeare's own writing of the later scene give equal colour to a more commonplace conception. This part of Act IV, Scene i, is intrinsically more Shakespearean than the earlier scenes in which the witches appear without Macbeth – though, truly, it is a weakness in criticism to be always maintaining that what is well done is by Shakespeare and what is ill done is by somebody else. This, however, is the more likely to be Shakespeare in that Holinshed's creatures for this particular purpose are 'certaine wizards' and 'a certaine witch.'[28] Yet Macbeth says that he will to the 'weird sisters.' It seems pretty clear that Shakespeare deliberately

---

[28] True, Shakespeare might have disregarded Holinshed here and Middleton, by a coincidence, have adhered to him. By coincidence, because he would hardly have deliberately rejected Shakespeare and yet sought Shakespeare's source. (Granville-Barker's note)

blended the two types. In the composite as we have it there is risk in claiming too much emphasis for the first. He may have continued to call them the weird sisters only because he had begun by calling them so. On the other hand, the part of their witchcraft that is essential to the play is given dignity and mystery, and it may be – it *may* be – that their incantations round the cauldron, which are given strength and good colour but no more, are, in form at least, Middleton's after all.

When it comes to their presentation on the stage one may perhaps proceed usefully by negation. Though they have supernatural powers, they are *not* supernatural beings. They are *not*, on the other hand, the sort of old women that Shakespeare may have seen ducked in the horse-pond at Stratford. And if his superstitious fancies on those occasions glorified such poor wretches somewhat, we should still be bound for stage purposes to consider a little what our fancies would confer on the same figures.

If we look, where we should usually look for a description, to the impression made upon some opposite character, to whom it is given to interpret an unusual figure to the audience, we find:

> . . . What are these
> So wither'd and so wild in their attire,
> That look not like th' inhabitants o' the earth
> And yet are on't?

and again:

> How now, you secret, black, and midnight hags!

And that surely paints them for us with sufficient clarity.

The last part of the play calls for the producer's very firm control of the elements that may otherwise, so to speak, run away with it. It is notable – though in the play's staging as a rule too little noticed – with what a very strong hand Shakespeare himself has controlled them. One need not again inveigh against the senseless omission from most productions of such a scene as that in which the revolted Scottish lords gather together, nor against the telescoping of those that picture Malcolm's advance. This misconduct alone tends to pile up the other part of the action into a lurid chaos and to make the strain on any player of Macbeth unbearable. But, right to the end, Shakespeare has most carefully balanced the horrible by the heroic. Young Siward's death and his father's fortitude is set against Macbeth's slaughtering and the uplifting of his severed head. And to wallow in the horror and omit the beauty and dignity is to degrade great tragedy to the depth of poor melodrama.

In character development Shakespeare has perhaps done all he can do — for his protagonists at least — even before the end of Act III. The rest is catastrophe, skilfully retarded. But in his marshalling of the play's action to its end, he surely outdoes even his own accustomed mastery in such matters. We have, in the scene with the weird sisters, the whipping up of the evil in Macbeth to the top of its fury, immediately followed by its most savage outbreak — sudden and short — upon Lady Macduff and the child. Then comes, as we have remarked, the elaborate and weighty preparation for the play's counter-action; an outspoken scene. In contrast to this follows the scene of sickness and whisperings and unnatural troubles, the scene of the slow perishing of one of the two evil beings of the play. Quickly after comes the gathering of the Scottish lords, like men escaping from prison and despair. The 'drum and colours' here strike a new note; lifted spirits are marked by such means as the rising inflection of Angus's second speech with its 'Now . . . Now . . . Now . . .'; and the repeated 'March we on' and 'Make we our march' begins the movement to the play's end.

Macbeth himself is, so to say, the fixed point towards which this movement sweeps. We are to see him at intervals, waiting the approach and desperate at having to wait, for this, as we know, was not his sort of soldiership. In the first of these scenes of his we have talk of preparation, but Shakespeare allows it none of the cheerful panoply of war, neither 'drum' nor 'colours.' Instead there is depression and distraction, the news of the flying of the Thanes, the terror of the 'cream-faced loon,' and, to clinch the effect, Macbeth's own contrariness about his armour — one of those simple touches that help to throw great issues into relief.

The following scene is so short that it is possible to give it the effect of an unhalting march. The Scottish and English armies are joined, their number is doubled. Malcolm has the leadership. But the last two voices are Macduff's and Siward's – to whom a very ringing speech is given, emphasis of his dignity and importance as the English general.

Now on Macbeth's side the martial note is sounded, and sounded loudly. This scene is more rhythmically written than his earlier one, and is meant to be more rapid. It has but two checks to its pace, the news of the Queen's death, and the couplet,

> I 'gin to be aweary of the sun;

and the latter may be designed to emphasise by contrast the rush of the end. The bringing of the news of the moving wood immediately upon the first reflective moment indicates an even greater contrast. At this point, if one were charting the scene as a fever is charted, one would show a perpendicular leap in energy. And the mere vocal effect of the passage beginning,

> Arm, arm, and out,

should be in itself an alarum bell.

Then follows, again, an interesting check and contrast. Malcolm's army is before Dunsinane, at rest for a moment. He and Siward coolly plan their battle. The trumpet-toned couplet at the end is given, for obvious reasons, to Macduff.

The actual conduct of the last scene upon Shakespeare's stage we have already discussed. Its inward scheme is not hard to determine, though, with so much movement involved, it may not be too easy to abide by in practice. It divides, dramatically, into three parts. The first runs to Macduff's discovery of Macbeth with

> Turn, hell-hound, turn.

This goes, as we say, ding-dong, and any possible half-pauses are filled up with 'alarums.' Macbeth is grim and deadly, a trapped beast; his comings and goings have no purpose in them. Moreover, as the battle goes forward he becomes conscious that his mind too has been trapped and tricked, though he cannot yet see how. He is invulnerable; again and again he returns to this. But, as certainly, with the battle against him, he is doomed. Is the answer to the riddle that he must kill himself? Must he 'play the Roman fool'? He fights, one would suppose, like an automaton and perhaps the more dangerously for that.

In clear contrast is the gallant, crusading figure of young Siward, flashing to his death.

There is none of the glow of battle upon Macduff. Methodically, determinedly, he pursues his single purpose. For a relief we have the interlude when the two generals, cool and confident still, enter the castle.

The second part concerns Macbeth and Macduff alone. Nice critics have found Macbeth's last fling of words — beloved of every schoolboy — too highly flavoured with bombast. They may be. But Shakespeare, having brought his play to the issue of sheer physical combat, might well think it appropriate to throw niceness behind him.[29] This is to be a mortal combat and a mighty combat. For Macduff to come easily by his vengeance would be unsatisfying. For Macbeth to go easily out would be incredible, and to give him a finely worded end might seem to redeem him, if ever so little. This Shakespeare will not do. He allows him one gleam of incorrigible pride, he leaves him his animal courage. For the rest, he sends him shouting to hell. And from the beginning the exchange of speeches between the two men should be like the exchange of blows.

The end of the play is contrived as a full and varied orchestra of voices with the trumpets of victory topping them. Malcolm and his soldiers enter processionally, and at once we are given the suggestion of order restored. The note of pity for the dead is struck, and upon it comes the practised soldier's stoic response. There is Rosse's smooth sympathy. There is the defiant nobility with which Siward takes his own son's death; and for Malcolm there is a needed touch of impulsive generosity.

Macduff's entrance, lifting the severed head, changes the key almost violently. Here is an echo of the now ended tragedy. Vengeance is accomplished, but Macduff, widowed and childless, stands apart from all thoughtless rejoicing.

---

[29] Not that he ever took much stock in it. (Granville-Barker's note)

I see thee compassed with thy kingdom's pearl.

But he is a man alone. His voice must have the music of a selfless and unforgettable sorrow in it.

Then, with the careful modulation of Malcolm's address to his people, Shakespeare brings us at his ease back to our work-a-day world.

Textual Variants

THE references are to the Arden edition – the *Macbeth* volume being edited by Henry Cuningham, – which is taken as a standard text.[30]

In general: omit all scene description. The scene division itself is sometimes quite arbitrary.

Act I, Scene i.	Spurious.
Scene ii.	For some remarks upon its general validity, see the body of this Preface.
21.	Cut 'which ne'er shook hands.' This at least will relieve the actor from talking nonsense.
45.	'*Enter Rosse.*' Restore '*and Angus*' from F1.
Scene iii.	Omit 1-36. For reasons, see body of the Preface.
68-9.	To be spoken by all three sisters, agreeably to Mr Cuningham's footnote. Incidentally, this is the theatrical tradition.
Scene vi.	For 'proposes' read 'purposes.' This is presumably a misprint in the Arden edition itself.
Act II, Scene i.	'*Enter Banquo*,' etc. 'Take thee that too'

---

[30] Nor should I forget to record the great use that Mr Cuningham's own notes have been to me, and my thanks for them. (Granville-Barker's note)

seems to imply that Banquo was carrying the torch, and had, besides Fleance, no torch-bearer with him. He could not conveniently carry the torch during the dialogue with Macbeth.

Scene iii, 92. '*Re-enter Macbeth and Lenox.*' Add '*and Rosse.*' This restoration of the F1 direction is important.

Act III, Sc. ii, 121. 'But wail his fall.' The 'But' is surely corrupt, and possibly the rest of the passage too. 'would' – see footnote – makes it a little better.

Scene iv, 74 & 107. '*Exit ghost*' after '*Enter ghost*' is quite adequate as a direction.

102. Put semicolon after 'blood,' and omit it after 'say.'

Scene v. Spurious.

Act IV, Sc. i, 39-47. Omit.

97. Read 'rebellion's head.'

124. Omit 'What! is this so?'

125-132. Omit. Direction to read '*Exeunt witches.*'

153-155. A good case can be made for the omission of 'No boasting . . . sights.' Its sense is pure repetition of 'From this moment . . . hand,' which comes but four lines earlier, and it smells strongly of Middleton.

Scene ii, 38-59. For retention *versus* omission, see the body of this Preface.

Act IV, Sc. iii, 236. 'God, God,' in place of 'Heaven,' if one might follow that authoritative emendation, would be a great strengthening.

Act V, Scene i, 35. Certainly, as the footnote claims, the punctuation of F1, with the full stop.

Scene v, 42. Read 'pall' for 'pull.'

'Preface' to The Tragedie of Macbeth, London, Ernest Benn Ltd., 1923, pp. xxv–lix. (The first volume of *The Players' Shakespeare*.)

NOTE: In a letter to Harcourt Williams, January 25, 1930, Granville-Barker says this 'Preface' is 'full of blunders' (quoted in C. B. Purdom, *Harley Granville Barker: Man of the Theatre, Dramatist and Scholar*, London: Rockliff Publishing Corp. Ltd., 1955, p. 234). See also the letter to Sir John Gielgud, October 27, 1940, printed *Ibid.*, p. 267.

Preface to
A Midsummer Night's Dream

PRE-EMINENTLY in three plays, in *A Midsummer Night's Dream, King Lear, Antony and Cleopatra,* Shakespeare's stage-craft is at issue with the mechanism of the modern theatre. It is an issue admitted, sometimes even perversely gloried in by editors; by the producer it is commonly evaded as far as may be. He has his modern audience to please and can plead this much excuse. But we in these prefaces must try at least to determine the issue and to analyse it, even though thereafter we can point to no solution but a compromise, and that an unsatisfactory one.

The issue for the three plays is not identical. In *King Lear* it is manifest in the greatness of the subject, in *Antony and Cleopatra* in the scope of the action. In *A Midsummer Night's Dream* it springs perhaps from the subject itself, more certainly from the necessities of its treatment as Shakespeare's stage determined them. Here is a play about fairies, about the adventures of four lovers and some rustics in a moonlit wood; and he wrote it for a theatre in which no visual illusion, as we interpret the term, was possible. His resource – all others beside it negligible – was the spoken word. No question of the wonders he works with this. Let us, however, with our modern theatre in mind, but before we yield to the charm of

> I know a bank where the wild thyme blows,
> Where oxlips and the nodding violet grows,
> Quite over-canopied with lush woodbine,
> With sweet musk-roses, and with eglantine :

and the rest – this magic stuff that Shakespeare pours not upon our eyes but in our ears – let us first note what he, very definitely, does *not* try to do.

We have grown accustomed to scenic productions of the play, and, of late years, almost as accustomed to protesting against them. And the dispute has apparently given birth to a perverse notion that we ought somehow to be able to make the best of both methods, that somewhere in Shakespeare's stagecraft the craft of the scenic stage is innate. This is surely a fallacy; does it need more than statement for its exposure?

> *Enter a fairy at one door and Robin Goodfellow at another,*

says the Folio. Shakespeare did not ask his audience to pretend to themselves that the doors were not there.

> Ill met by moonlight, proud Titania.

He did not expect them to shut their eyes upon the plain stage and visualise a moonlit glade.

He avoids the incongruous:

> I know a bank where the wild thyme blows.

It is not a bank which ought at that moment to be within sight and obviously isn't. No, our eyes may make sure of whatever is actually in front of them; Oberon in a fantastic dress, Puck bounding through a palpable doorway with his little western flower. For the rest – for how much, then! – the appeal is as directly to the ear as the appeal of a song or a symphony.

But to-day we are accustomed to the theatre of visual illusion. True, it is not deception we demand: at the age of ten or thereabout we cease to ask, 'Are they real trunks of trees?' The liking for make-believe lasts longer. 'So this is the forest of Arden.' Give us something that can be called ocular proof of it, if we are to give whole-hearted credit to Touchstone and Rosalind. But finally our need is aesthetic. The eye must be occupied and satisfied. It has been taught how to add its gains to the sum of the emotion a play can excite, and it has grown exigent. If it is not satisfied, it will turn traitor and frustrate the other senses.

But can we dress Shakespeare in a garment, however delightful, for which he made no allowance without cramping his play's action and obscuring its beauty? There has been much quarrel-

ling round the question, between those who protest against any
garment at all and those who are all for a garment, but at odds
with each other – and most bitterly – as to the sort of garment
it should be. The case against realistic scenery is a good one and
never better than when this play is made the instance of it. Are
we first to have Shakespeare's verse paint us the bank of wild
thyme, nodding violet and musk-rose, and then let the scene-
painter take his turn and show us a pretty picture so like the
real thing that, 'By Jove,' we whisper (and while we whisper
our distracted neighbours miss half a dozen lines of the play),
'you could almost pick those violets, couldn't you?' It will be
admitted that to bring competing and discordant elements into
the interpretation of any work of art is wrong. To avoid discord-
ancy while satisfying still that hungry eye, modern producers
have devised scenery which is not scenery, forests that are not
like forests, and light that never was on sea or land. But have
they thereby eliminated the competition too? That part of the
question, in all its implications, is not so easy to answer, nor
will the problem as a whole yield to logic. There are three
parties to a dramatic performance, and each has its rights (and
the scene-painter, if he is to be admitted, may make a fourth).
The playwright devises, the actors interpret, and the rights of
the audience are to a language of word and movement, which
they can currently understand. Where all concerned are in
familiar touch, no difficulty should arise. But in three hundred
years even the theatre has seen changes. Shakespeare stands at
one end of a road that has many turnings, and we at the other.
He offers and asks for one thing; we are ready enough to offer
and like another. How far will the new thing supplement the
old, how far does it nullify it – that, roughly, is what one has
to discover. In this play, for instance, he asks attention for his
verse, for a little music, and allows for the eye only some simple
costumed action and a little dancing upon a palpable stage. With
these materials, within these bounds, his faculties at full stretch,
he produces his play. Using these materials, kept within those
bounds, and stretching our faculties of interpretation and appreciation to their full, we still – it is barely possible – may not be
able to compass his vision and achieve his purposes, limited as
they were. Change the materials, enlarge the bounds, and shall

we not lose rather than gain? May not the beauty of a setting belittle the actor who is seen in it? Is the ear not cheated by delighting the eye? For the eye responds more easily, people look before they listen, we are naturally lazy, and our total faculty of attention is limited.

> Dark night that from the eye his function takes
> The ear more quick of apprehension makes.

The play itself has something to say upon the point.[1]

On the other hand here is our modern audience to be considered, with its justified demand for the use of conventions to which it is accustomed. The nearer we can all come, by use or study, to Shakespeare's own understanding of his art the better – that should be obvious. But the play, once it starts, must be so ordered as to yield us spontaneous enjoyment, even as it did – by conventions to which they were accustomed – to the audiences of three centuries ago.[2]

Here, then, is the issue and the producer's problem. This differs, of course, but in degree, not in kind, from that which every other play of Shakespeare must present to the modern stage. It is, by all appearances, the harder to solve, but, paradoxically, it may prove the more perfectly solvable. For, treat this play how you will, there is none whose interpretation must so much depend upon that unchartered individual quality we call taste. Perhaps Shakespeare's own production was a failure. He wrote no more of fairies, and he was not above trying to improve on a success. But it will be wise not to rely too much upon that possibility. And one piece of practical advice may be offered. Let the producer first bring his work to completion

---

[1] There may even be a deep disharmony in an attempt to respond with sight and hearing simultaneously to any purely *emotional* appeal. In the theatre, of course, the two senses are under intellectual guidance – or should be. But this may be what is wrong – and there is something fundamentally wrong – with modern opera. (Granville-Barker's note)

[2] Not that conventions (in the theatre or elsewhere) are necessarily such rigid things as, untested, they may seem. Often we are unconsciously weary of them and ready enough to adopt a new one. By a little coaxing a lost one may be revived. By boldness the most formidable may sometimes be simply neglected. It is a producer's business to discern which – for his immediate purposes – have aesthetic validity and which have none. (Granville Barker's note)

upon Shakespeare's own terms, and none other. If he can perfect the music of the poetry and the grace of the play's movement, not so much else will need doing. And in this preface we shall be concerned only with the play as Shakespeare's theatre might have staged it. The rest of the adventure, if it must be made, is a man's own affair. But when he had given the last inch of energy demanded, and devoted his imagination single-mindedly to Shakespeare's service, he should be aware enough of his author's purpose not, for the rest, to go so far wrong, one may suppose.

The Text and Act-Division

There are no important difficulties in the text; only a number of tiresome trifles have to be passed upon.[3] Some few emendations force themselves upon us. But temptation merely to regularise the verse, where chance offers, had mostly better be resisted. The printer lapsed from full accuracy now and then, no doubt. But Shakespeare, even by this time, had come to prefer a dramatic effect, if only a tiny one, to a correctly rounded line.

The five act division is hardly a convenient one, if acts are to imply intervals and an audience going and coming. But there is this incidental interest in it. A stage-direction for the lovers, *They sleepe all the act* – that is, they remain asleep upon the stage during the interval between Acts III and IV – supplies us with one of the few pieces of evidence as to what an act-pause in the Elizabethan theatre might (but not by any means 'must') mean. If the actors lay there, it stands to reason that the interval, on this occasion, was not a very long one.

This carries us further. Act IV is short, but Act III is the longest of the five, and the two together make a large slice of the play. Therefore if they were played practically together, it is some sign, at least, that Elizabethan audiences were not hungry for intervals as we understand them. Perhaps they strolled in and out, intervals or no. The five act division had classic sanc-

---

[3] These are dealt with, as usual, at the preface's end. (Granville-Barker's note)

tion. Whether the editors of the Folio imposed it on Shakespeare to lend him academic respectability, whether Shakespeare himself had, at times, or invariably, formally accepted it, scholars have not determined.[4] Our question, however, with the play's production involved, need only be: what dramatic validity have these divisions, do they rightly define the structure of the play?

A case can be made out for them. But then, with a method at once so flowing and so discursive as the Elizabethan stage allowed, half a dozen different plans for dividing up any play can be allowed dramatic purpose, and defended. Act I as it stands is a unit of action, plainly enough; so is Act V. But there is as good a dramatic case for a pause after Act III, Scene i, as at the end of Act II. Again, a pause after Act III may be effective; but, as we have seen, it is, on an Elizabethan stage, technically inconvenient. And if, with the resources of the modern stage to rely upon, this consideration is to be ruled out, then a pause – on the whole as effective in itself, and dramatically far more purposeful – could be made after Oberon, Titania and Puck depart in the middle of Act IV, Scene i. Modern producers, as it happens, see at this point – and generally take – an opportunity for a prolonged sunrise to slow music while the lovers and Bottom lie sleeping. For the music they may plead Shakespeare; though if, as is possible, the lovers had slept 'all the act' to a musical accompaniment but a few minutes earlier, he is unlikely to have repeated the effect. But an interval, falling here, would leave a most inadequate fourth act, which is short even as it now stands.

And so one can argue, in this play as in others, for and against this division and that. The general conclusion will be, one may suggest, that on the Elizabethan stage the act-division

[4] Such an interval as the Folio directs between Acts III and IV of this play I call formal acceptance. By it the dramatist marks a certain rhythm in the play's action. An interval, in which an audience disperses or talks, has a further importance. In a modern theatre this relaxing of attention, the breaking of the spell of emotion, an opportunity to make the passing of time seem more valid, are things to be seriously considered. How far these things affected Elizabethan audiences it is hard to say. But it is hard to believe that playwrights would remain insensible to the dramatic gain or loss that might be involved. (Granville-Barker's note)

was a matter of practical convenience. Shakespeare constructed a play according to a certain plan, or at least developed it to some rhythm. He may sometimes – perhaps in *King Lear,* in *Antony and Cleopatra* – have had the classic five-act form in mind; oftener there is intrinsic evidence that he had not. It is possible that in the theatres four formal pauses were made. When intervals as we understand them were in question, it is as possible that these were let depend upon convenience for the shifting of properties, the changing of costumes, the doubling of parts, and the like. Moreover there is evidence that, if a play were shifted from one type of stage to another, intervals (and even formal pauses, therefore) might, for convenience' sake, be redistributed, rhythm of construction and dramatic effect being counted as of not much importance or held to be not much affected in the process.

This, if it be allowed, should at least free the modern producer from any sort of slavery to the five acts of the Folio. He must then abide by whatever rhythm of construction he divines in the play; and 'the fewer intervals the better' is a good general rule with a play that needs to transport its audiences into a mood of fancy and to hold them there, yet does not strain their emotions. Much is to be said with this play for treating Act I as a prelude, then for giving Acts II, III, IV with no break. Act V has every claim to stand separate, though the second scene of Act IV can, if convenient, be quite legitimately tacked to it.

Nor need the producer concern himself, in this connection, with the play's 'time analysis,' upon which thought and ink have been wasted in plenty. The duration of the action is planned for four days. This is stated to begin with, and so emphatically stated that we are obviously meant to remark it. And the dramatic worth of the matter lies, of course, in the need for giving Hermia some clearly stated and limited time in which to make choice of her fate. Shakespeare knows the value of a firm jumping-off place. Thereafter the matter loses its importance for him, and he becomes – we may disrespectfully surmise – correspondingly careless about its regulation. The adventures in the wood are *in effect* the adventures of one night. When Theseus wakes the lovers, he states that the four days are up – and who is there that would contradict such a benevolent hero? Nor does it matter to Hermia, for her troubles are over. Nor does the audience notice a discrepancy, nor did Shakespeare care, nor need the play's producer.

The Staging

We can extract from the text and the directions one or two bits of evidence as to the play's staging in Shapespeare's time; they may help to show the modern producer when it will and will not prove yielding to the importunity of his own circumstances.

There is a story that the play was written to be performed at some great marriage festivity. What a wedding present! And – though the text as we have it may show addition – the story is a likely one. There is the fitness of the fable, the play's whole tone and atmosphere, the appropriate ending. Further, there are small signs of some later adaptation to the public stage.[5] Between Acts III and IV comes that stage-direction for the lovers, *They sleepe all the act.* No such direction is given for Titania between Acts II and III. Why? Possibly – probably! – because her bower was the inner stage and could be concealed throughout an interval with curtains.[6] But that sleeping *all the act* is a clumsy business, whose-ever the responsibility for it. The lovers must lie on the outer, the open stage. They cannot be crowded together; besides, the inner stage will be needed a dozen lines later. But it does not look as if any dramatist would in his play's first planning have let himself and his actors in for such an awkward few minutes.

Right upon this comes:

Enter Queen of Fairies, and Clowne, and Fairies, and the King behind them

---

[5] Some of these signs, being noted, have been interpreted as evidence of the play's original writing for a public theatre, the adaptation being for Court or wedding performance. But the Folio text is, hardly disputably, that of a prompt copy; and the stage-directions – for me the important evidence – are less likely to belong to a special performance than to the current practice of its acting. Though, again, this may, latterly, have been at a 'private' theatre – to which on all counts the play is better suited – rather than a public one. (Granville-Barker's note)

[6] This, of course, would be consistent with the play's original writing for the stage of a public theatre. (Granville-Barker's note)

According to the Quartos Oberon remains behind them till Bottom is asleep, when Puck enters to him; according to the Folio he must go off at some unstated moment, for we have

Enter Robin Goodfellow and Oberon.

What is the point of the change? Probably that, the exposition of sleep having come upon him, Bottom must be retired to the inner stage, or he will be sadly in the way when Theseus and Hippolyta appear and wake the lovers. Oberon, therefore, cannot stay *behind them.* But when the Quarto copy was made he could.

There is like evidence in Act III, Scene i, of some change in the circumstances of staging, and again Titania's bower is concerned. Part of the confusion may be due to the printer's errors. But it does look as if the apparition of Bottom with the ass-head did not at first involve his entrance; and is there – or not – a peculiar insistence upon 'this hawthorn brake'?

These are flimsy matters upon which to found any theory. But now consider the play's construction as a whole. No use is made, except thus confusedly, of the ordinary stage resources of a public theatre. Picture, on the other hand, the great hall of an Elizabethan mansion, with the two doors in the screen at its end. These provide exit and entrance enough.[7] Imagine such a 'machine' as was commonly used for masques, carried in or pushed forward for the fairy scenes to serve as a hawthorn brake and Titania's bower, carried out or pushed back when they were over; imagine some 'banks' disposed around for the lovers to sleep on, and chairs and benches brought in for the audience of the 'most lamentable comedy.' Into such a setting it will be found that the general action of the play and even its detailed business most conveniently fit.

Not that we are called upon to-day to reproduce these exact circumstances even if they were those of its original production.

---

[7] The stage arrangements at the 'private' theatres are still matters of discussion, and they may have approximated to this. But then the play's date comes into the question. If it was written for Shakespeare's company, where was it played if not either at their public theatre or in a private hall? (Granville-Barker's note)

But they may suggest to us the particular kinds of effect that Shakespeare looked for in the play's interpretation.

The 'machine' gave no illusion, that goes without saying. It was a pretty, perhaps fantastic piece of decoration, which enabled Titania to lie hid while other scenes passed, from which, possibly, Bottom protruded his ass-head to the terror of his fellows, who were so innocently regarding their tiring house, expecting his re-entry from it. And its exchange for the inner stage or for whatever substitute a modern theatre may provide need make little more than mechanical difference. But what will count for far more will be the intimacy of the whole affair and the qualities of performance which intimacy allows and makes effective. And this is worth more than passing consideration. There is no play of Shakespeare's that demands (the clowns' scenes apart, and even these should be simply done) such sustained delicacy of treatment. Story and characters both are kept — are constantly being reined — within the bounds of gentleness. The verse has the virtues of chamber music. It is never robustly declamatory; it asks constantly for a quiet clarity of utterance; it offers chance after chance for the most delicate phrasing. And nothing can compensate for the lack or the loss of all this. There are no opportunities for vigorous acting as the Elizabethans understood it, and violence, assertiveness, any mere noise will break the whole fabric. Egeus is allowed to create no more than will provide a lively contrast to Duke Theseus' magnanimity (and serve as a warning to stern parents in the audience not to make themselves ridiculous when love-affairs are in hand). Puck's boisterousness is but that of a naughty child. The four-handed lovers' quarrel is turned to amusing futility. But we have:

> . . . O happy fair,
> Your eyes are lodestars and your tongue's sweet air,
> More tuneable than lark to shepherd's ear,
> When wheat is green, when hawthorn buds appear.
>
> Fair love, you faint with wandering in the wood;
> And to speak troth, I have forgot our way;
> We'll rest us, Hermia, if you think it good,
> And tarry for the comfort of the day.

Be kind and courteous to this gentleman;
Hop in his walks, and gambol in his eyes;
Feed him with apricocks, and dewberries,
With purple grapes, green figs, and mulberries;
The honey-bags steal from the humble-bees,
And, for night-tapers, crop their waxen thighs,
And light them at the fiery glow-worm's eyes,
To have my love to bed, and to arise;
And pluck the wings from painted butterflies,
To fan the moon-beams from his sleeping eyes :
Nod to him, elves, and do him courtesies.

     . . . damned spirits all,
That in cross-ways and floods have burial,
Already to their wormy beds are gone;
For fear lest day should look their shames upon,
They wilfully themselves exile from light,
And must for aye consort with black-brow'd night.
But we are spirits of another sort;
I with the morning's love have oft made sport;
And, like a forester, the groves may tread,
Even till the eastern gate, all fiery-red,
Opening on Neptune with fair blessed beams,
Turns into yellow gold his salt green streams.

My hounds are bred out of the Spartan kind,
So flew'd, so sanded; and their heads are hung
With ears that sweep away the morning dew;
Crook-knee'd, and dew-lapp'd like Thessalian bulls;
Slow in pursuit, but match'd in mouth like bells,
Each under each.

Wherever and however the play was first performed, whether
by candelight to a kindly company – to just such a company as
Duke Theseus himself would have gathered into just such a
hall – or whether it did first face the daylight and distraction
of a public theatre, such verse must gain by gracious treatment
and response, even as the music of stringed instruments is
mellowed in an old panelled room.

The Music and Dancing

For long, Mendelssohn's music to the play, charming in itself, seemed to have acquired a prescriptive right to be used. But, apart from the question of intrinsic suitability, it involves a quite unallowable treatment of the text; involves, besides, the practical suppression of the lyrics. 'You spotted snakes,' for instance, might be written in German or Choctaw for any sense that the cleverest singer of it to this music can make for the keenest listener.

The whole problem, Mendelssohn dismissed, has been argued acutely and with authority by Mr Cecil Sharp, who, moreover, was able to put his conclusions very successfully to the test. He decided for folk-song and dance, though it must be owned that his arguments might well have led another man elsewhere. Country dance, however, if not folk-dance, is thrust on us by the text, by Titania's

> If you will patiently dance in our round . . .
> Come now a roundel, and a fairy song.

Nor is the ditty which is to be sung and danced by the light of the dead and drowsy fire likely to differ greatly from this. And a bergomask is a bergomask.

But as to the music itself, Mr Sharp broaches the question of music for Shakespeare's plays in general,[8] and it is over this that though diffidently, I must join issue with him. He suggests three possible methods of providing it; of these rejects, first, the adaptation of Elizabethan music originally set to other words, second, the composing of music in the Elizabethan idiom, and prefers original composition. He does so on the broad ground that though 'Shakespeare the man was an Elizabethan; Shakespeare the artist and the dramatist belongs to all time,' and says that 'To us Elizabethan music always sounds

---

[8] In his preface to *Music for A Midsummer Night's Dream*, Simpkin, Marshall, 1914. (Granville-Barker's note) This book, of course, was for Granville-Barker's production. The correct title is: *The Songs and Incidental Music Arranged and Composed for Granville Barker's Production of A Midsummer Night's Dream at the Savoy Theatre in January, 1914.*

strange, unfamiliar, archaic – and, to some extent, precious.'

It seems such wholesome doctrine that one is loth to reject it. But, in practice, will not the modern musician, thus encouraged to 'be himself,' be to Shakespeare very much what most other modern collaborators have been, working by such encouragement; – painters, limelighters, costumiers, crying out, 'Not for an age, but for all time,' and smothering him with their enthusiastic contributions to his glory? Now and then one might find a composer, the quality of whose art, its values of emotion and form, had about that relation to Shakepeare's own for which he allowed in the nicely calculated opportunities he gave for collaboration between the two. Shakespeare knew something about music, it appears; he had, at least, rather more than a 'reasonable good ear for the tongs and bones.' We must suppose therefore that he imagined, pretty justly, the precise quality that was to be produced when Oberon began,

> Come, my Queen, take hands with me,
> And rock the ground whereon these sleepers be,

and to be produced almost as much by the accompanying music as the words themselves.

Music, even as Drama, has developed new resources and found new methods in three hundred years. One does Shakespeare ill service by setting his plays in visual surroundings which, being designed for other modes of dramatic expression, necessarily deform them. Is it much better to blanket them with sounds as foreign?

If, as Mr Sharp says, Elizabethan music *does* sound archaic and too unfamiliar to the modern ear, then, by the sound plea that a play must provide spontaneous enjoyment, there is a case for compromise between past and present – though this may but lead us to his rejected (wisely rejected, as I think) composing of music in Elizabethan idiom. But the letting loose of modern musicians with a recommendation to do their damn'dest will, for the moment, almost certainly result in tyrannous noise. I should myself have thought (though necessarily in such a matter I speak under correction) that here, precisely, was an opportunity for leading an audience back, and all unconsciously, into that medium of sound, of emotion even, in which the play was first meant to make its effect. It is just because Elizabethan music *is* somewhat unfamiliar to the ear that I advocate it. It will not surely strike the uninstructed hearer so strangely as to provoke argument or raise questions; and the instructed hearer can probably take the appropriate sort of pleasure in it. Music affects most of us without our well knowing why. Moreover there is no art that can so readily, by suggestion, and even by its very unfamiliarity, transport us over time and space, though the destination be barely known. Bagpipes suggest Scotland, a guitar Italy, a tomtom the jungle. A minuet will set us imagining eighteenth-century surroundings. We may lack the knowledge to place Byrd and Dowland in theirs, but the surroundings in this case are supplied by the play. We have only to surrender to the sounds.

Music, truly, is of its time; and there is innate in it something of the spirit and behaviour of its time, which could never perhaps find equal expression in words. Words are for thoughts, and emotion must be framed in terms of thought before words will convey it. But music may express something, now as simple as set movements of the body, now as subtle as those moods of the mind and the measures to which emotion learns to beat. By reasoning about it we may make it more strange than it ever need be if we simply listen. For the emotional self is apter at shifting ground than the intellectual, apter to explode unknown ground.[9] I am sure at least that you can sing and dance a man back into the seventeenth century far more easily than you can argue him there. And I cannot think that any approach to listening with Shakespeare's ears is other than a gain. One of the ways to a love of his verse may well be through the music that he loved.

For *A Midsummer Night's Dream* itself, however, Mr Sharp finds a fourth plan which does not conflict with my theories and (he will forgive me) saves him the application of his own. He chooses folk-music — 'which is impervious to the passage of time and will satisfy equally the artistic ideals of every age . . . It is undated, it belongs to no period; it is a growth, not a composi-

---

[9] And if there is such a thing as racial memory, music, one would say, could be counted on to call it to life. (Granville-Barker's note)

tion.' From pure liking I agree that for the fairy roundels, Bottom's courageous carolling, and for the Bergomask nothing better can be found than folk-music. It has its roots in the ages; it must have sounded familiarly in Shakespeare's ears, as it still, at first hearing, sounds somehow familiar to us. One might pedantically call its use for Oberon's 'still music' into question, but unity of effect will excuse this. For other plays, though, folk-music will not serve; and then Mr Sharp and I must find ourselves at honest odds.

Two particular points need remark. The fairy song for the last scene is missing; of that there is little doubt, and somehow one must be supplied. The expedient (Mendelssohn's) of setting Oberon's and Titania's two speeches to music instead is a poor one, and Capell is surely right when he condemns the Folio's printing of Oberon's speech, 'Now until the break of day,' following the song as the song itself. The producer, therefore, in his difficulty will search Shakespeare for another appropriate lyric. If he cannot find one (and I think he cannot), he must turn, as it may be Shakespeare did, elsewhere. It so happens, however, that a play with which Shakespeare's own name has been traditionally associated, *The Two Noble Kinsmen,* has in it a wedding song not unlike his own work, nor quite unworthy of him.

> Roses, their sharp spines being gone,
> Not royal in their smell alone
>   But in their hue;
> Maiden pinks, of odour faint,
> Daisies smell-less, yet most quaint,
>   And sweet thyme true;
>
> Primrose, firstborn child of Ver,
> Merry spring-time's harbinger
>   With her bells dim;
> Ox-lips in their cradles growing,
> Marigolds on deathbeds blowing,
>   Larks'-heels trim.
>
> All dear Nature's children sweet,
> Lie 'fore bride and bridegroom's feet,
>   Blessing their sense!

Not an angel of the air,
Bird melodious or bird fair,
   Be absent hence!

The crow, the slenderous cuckoo, nor
The boding raven, nor chough hoar,
   Nor chattering pie,
May on our bride-house perch or sing,
Or with them any discord bring,
   But from it fly!

In default of better this may serve.[10]

The *Musicke Tongs, Rurall Musicke* of the Folio (Act IV, Scene i) may fairly be held suspect. Not to speak of its absence from the Quartos, the run of the text here almost forbids any such interruption. The only likely occasion for it is when Peas-

---

[10] Mr Richmond Noble, in his *Shakespeare's Use of Song*, holds that the song is not missing, and that 'Now until the break of day' and the twenty-two following lines *are* the song. I venture to disagree. The passage does not (but for the last three lines) differ in metre from much of the verse that is certainly meant to be spoken, as one would expect a lyric written for singing to do. Dramatically the context, Titania's

    Will we sing and bless this place?
and Oberon's

    Now, until the break of day
suggest a gap that some song has filled. Why 'Now,' otherwise? And if Mr Noble's instinct, as he says — his musical instinct? — informs him that this passage is to be sung, my dramatic instinct suggests that its speaking by Oberon will give his part an ending commensurate with its importance. Singing alone might not detract from this, even though Oberon did little of the singing; but a ditty sung and danced certainly will. But then Mr Noble considers that

    Through the house give glimmering light
'must be either sung or intoned, otherwise the ascending value of the words cannot be adequately conveyed.' Could not as good reasons be found for treating half a dozen other passages in the same fashion? And are we not then on the road back to Mendelssohn's *recitative* for

    That very night I saw, but thou couldst not . . .?
Incidentally Mr Noble condemns the use of

    Roses, their sharp spines being gone,
and denies it to Shakespeare. Upon the point of authorship I am no judge. But if its length is against it (one reason given), it is only one line longer than 'Now until the break of day' would be. And I should not have thought — speaking, again, under correction — that the opening phrases could be much more difficult to sing (another reason) than

    You spotted snakes with double tongue,
    Thorny hedgehogs be not seen, etc.,
must prove. (Granville-Barker's note)

blossom and company have been dismissed. There would be a pleasing, fantastic irony in little Titania and her monster being lulled to sleep by the distant sound of the tongs and the bones; it would make a properly dramatic contrast to the 'still music' for which she calls a moment later, her hand in Oberon's again. A producer might, without offence, venture on the effect. (But Oberon, by the way, had better stop the noise with a disgusted gesture before he begins to speak.)

And the winding of the horns that follows should be quite elaborately symphonic. This is Shakepeare's picturing of sunrise.

The Costume

A designer finds himself with a fairly free hand; and the freer he keeps it, within the bounds of discretion, the better. He should not, that is to say, let himself be entrapped by the word 'Athens' into any chilly and so-called classical precision. Duke Theseus has no closer relation to his historical namesake than has Oberon to Louis Quatorze. The sounding names Hippolyta Perigenia, Ariadne, the talk of Diana's altar and of hounds of Sparta, and of coming a conqueror from Thebes, were still romantic in Elizabethan ears and called up figures moving in some 'once upon a time.' Does our imagination respond differently to-day? Can we not hear

> Call Philostrate.
> Here, mighty Theseus.
> Say what abridgement have you for this evening?
> What masque? what music? . .

without the classic names obliterating the Elizabethan phrase? Well, let the figures of the two, as we are to see them staged, allow as much for our susceptibilities as will not mean the re-drawing or discolouring of the imaginative picture of the play as it was first made. Here is the designer's problem, so far as one exists. He will further have to contrive some unity of effect. For Oberon and Titania are, it appears, as at home in India as in Athens. Puck begins to smack of Warwickshire. And though Quince and his fellows may work for bread upon Athenian stalls, as we hear them talk it does not seem as if they would be strangers, quite, in Stratford market-place.

The Casting and Acting

The cast falls roughly into three groups: that of Theseus and the lovers, the fairies, the clowns. To the first two falls the speaking of the verse; for this purpose they must be thought of together.

While it would be misleading to speak of a musical range of voices wanted, from *basso* for Theseus to *soprano* for Titania, – for that would be to formalise the matter unduly to the prejudice of individual character – nevertheless one should have in mind some such structure of tone. In any play it will count as a means of marking its form, of giving contrast between part and part, and of making scene succeeding scene the fresher to the ear. And in this play it will count more than in most.

Hints – fortuitously dropped, no doubt – of the importance Shakespeare might attach to a characteristic quality of voice and to beauty of speech generally are not lacking in the plays. Lear's tribute to Cordelia is in everyone's mind. Part of Helena's prettily envious praise of her rival is of a

> tongue's sweet air,
> More tuneable than lark to shepherd's ear.

And the very tone in which Hippolyta must tell us that once in a wood of Crete she bay'd the boar with hounds of Sparta till

> . . . every region near
> Seem'd all one mutual cry: I never heard
> So musical a discord, such sweet thunder;

and Theseus' answer that his hounds are

> . . . match'd in mouth like bells,
> Each under each,

– the very words seem to suggest such matching of their own tones.[11] But no hints should be needed to tell us how vital is this question of right relation between the voices. One must beware

---

[11] Not to mention that Bottom undertakes to roar us as gentle as any sucking dove! (Granville-Barker's note)

of pushing the comparison with music too far; but to neglect this would be as if one should leave the parts in a symphony to the lot of any instruments that might come handy.

Take the very first scene. It opens with the formal serenity of Theseus' and Hippolyta's speeches; mellow-toned — note the sounds of the vowels in

> Now, fair Hippolyta, our nuptial hour
> Draws on apace.

Impinging on this comes the shrill rattle of Egeus with his

> . . . rings, gawds, conceits,
> Knacks, trifles, nosegays, sweet-meats; . . .

Next, Hermia's meek obstinacy, rhythmical, distinct, low:

> I do entreat your grace to pardon me.
> I know not by what power I am made bold;
> Nor how it may concern my modesty,
> In such a presence here to plead my thoughts.

Then Demetrius and Lysander strike each his note. Demetrius, slow, hard-bitten, positive, pleasantly surly — not much romance in this young man.

> Relent, sweet Hermia; — and, Lysander, yield
> Thy crazed title to my certain right.

And Lysander, glib and impertinent, melodious, light:

> You have her father's love, Demetrius;
> Let me have Hermia's : do you marry him.

Fine spirit in him too, though; for he says his say to the Duke, bates not a point of it, rings it out confident and clear. The measured speech and mellow voice of Theseus now modulate the scene back to the tone it began upon. Then he departs with his train and the lovers are left alone.

The passage which follows must be one of the most charming things that Shakespeare ever wrote. It is besides (such appraisement being somewhat profitless) typical of the play in quality and method both; better than charming, it is typically right.

LYSANDER. How now, my love? Why is your cheek so pale?
　　　How chance the roses there do fade so fast?
HERMIA. Belike for want of rain; which I could well
　　　Beteem them from the tempest of mine eyes.
LYSANDER. Ah me! for aught that ever I could read,
　　　Could ever hear by tale or history,
　　　The course of true love never did run smooth!
　　　But, either it was different in blood;
HERMIA. O cross! too high to be enthrall'd to low!
LYSANDER. Or else misgraffed, in respect of years;
HERMIA. O spite! too old to be engag'd to young!
LYSANDER. Or else it stood upon the choice of friends:
HERMIA. O hell! to choose love by another's eye!
LYSANDER. Or, if there were a sympathy in choice,
　　　War, death, or sickness did lay siege to it;
　　　Making it momentary as a sound,
　　　Swift as a shadow, short as any dream;
　　　Brief as the lightning in the collied night,
　　　That, in a spleen, unfolds both heaven and earth,
　　　And ere a man hath power to say, — Behold!
　　　The jaws of darkness do devour it up:
　　　So quick bright things come to confusion.

The whole passage is conventional in form. Conceit answers conceit. The pretty antiphony is convention itself. Lysander's apologue is conventionally rounded and complete. But how nicely it is charged with emotion, with enough to illumine the form, but not with so much, nor of such a complexity as would warp it. Hence it is dramatically right; that is to say, the matter and manner are at one.

Note the intimate tenderness to which Lysander's first bravado has turned. The two are alone in a yet unfriendly world. Not a tragic world though, for Theseus had straightway suggested the softening of the rebellious young lady's punishment — at the worst to a vowing of austerity and single life. They can be playfully wistful about their hard fate. And as the scene ripples on, Hermia springs to cheerfulness as delicately as she had fallen to grief; the way out is so easy; in a minute she is bantering her lover.

Now comes Helena, wistful and troubled in her turn, her first speech matching Lysander's plaint of the course of true love.

Another antiphony to follow, lightly comic this time, Hermia chirping her disdainful triumph, Helena drooping to defeated silence. Then, one at each side, the two lovers start to cheer Helena with the tale of their own good luck to be, their thoughts and voices alike in tune. Oblivious of her silence they go their ways; and she is left to protest, prettily, fancifully and spiritedly – there being no target near now for her humility – of her fate, and to flash on a plan not of happiness, but of the next best thing, of an even better thing for the purposes of comedy, redoubled woe. So the scene ends.

It is ill anatomising such delicate stuff – the dissection of a butterfly! But this is how butterfly flights must be achieved in the theatre, where nothing is natural that is not made first by study, then by forgetfulness, to appear so.

Well, what does the dissection first serve to show? To say that the sense of the scene springs from its sound would, of course, be absurd. But it is remarkable how much sheer sound, in quality, contrast, change, is made to contribute. Make as much of the stark meaning of it all as you will; if the scene is sung to the wrong tunes (the comparison is, for once, irresistible), if the time is not adjusted, if the discords and harmonies are not valued, its essential character will be obscured and lost. This must be to some extent true of any play; in the interpretation of *A Midsummer Night's Dream* it is the dominating truth. For Shakespeare has sacrificed every other more purely dramatic advantage to this one. He allows himself no absorbing complexity of plot, no development of character. Nothing – it was his mood – may mar or cloud the limpid music of his verse. Development of character, indeed, his scheme in any case forbids. There can be little of it under enchantment. Human promptings do certainly bring the lovers to the wood, but once there they are spell-bound. No one but Oberon remains master of himself, and fairy psychology would seem to be of the simplest.[12] But is it not all meant to appear only as the fierce

---

[12] It could be pedantically argued that neither Hermia's nor Helena's eyes were anointed with the love-juice; they, therefore, might have behaved just a little more sensibly. This only shows the danger of ever starting to argue about *A Midsummer Night's Dream*. (Granville-Barker's note)

vexation of a dream? Even so — even within these limits — Shakespeare forswears the strong contrasts of personality which are the stepping stones of a play's progress and can make the conflict of its scenes more forcible. He has occasion, that is to say, for the merely fantastic incongruity of Bottom wound in Titania's arms. But, having once outlined his Hermia and Helena, Demetrius and Lysander, he makes little enough play with their likeness or unlikeness till he needs some material for fun in a squabble.

Nor does the verse itself, as a rule, hold any extreme effects of light and shade. It has neither sharp turns of phrase, nor sudden checking of pace, nor one twisted or tortured thought. It flows on like a river in sunlight. When a particular effect is wanted we are more likely to find it made by purely poetic means. We have the change to a tenser metre for Puck and Oberon when the magic of the love-juice is in question, or when Puck is dancing with suppressed excitement. We have the pretty use of a quatrain to emphasise the drowsy happiness in which Hermia and Lysander wander through the wood; the use of quatrain and couplet and a four times repeated rhyme when there is need to stress the increasing delusion of the lovers — this sudden pleasant artificiality does somehow help to.

In fine, Shakespeare has a theme, which only poetry can fully illuminate, and he trusts to poetry. Nor will he risk any conflict of interest, all the rest of his dramatist's equipment must cry small for the occasion. Wherefore we in our turn must plan the play's interpretation upon these terms. Poetry, poetry; everything to serve and nothing to compete with it!

Should Oberon and Titania differ from the mortals by any trick of speech?[13] Shakespeare has made little provision for it. He allots, as we have seen, a small amount of short metre verse to them and to Puck. There is in thus much strangeness a certain suggestion of their fairy status, and it is to be noted that after their reconciliation to the sound of the 'still music' comes

---

[13] By 'trick,' needless to say, I, in no case, mean to imply anything 'tricky.' (Granville-Barker's note)

PUCK. Fairy king, attend, and mark;
    I do hear the morning lark.
OBERON. Then, my queen, in silence sad,
        Trip we after the night's shade:
        We the globe can compass soon,
        Swifter than the wand'ring moon.
TITANIA. Come, my lord; and in our flight,
        Tell me how it came this night,
        That I sleeping here was found
        With these mortals, on the ground.

The lilt, no less than the meaning, helps to express them to us as beings other than mortal, treading the air. And still more significant, of course, is the use of the same metre when they come with their train to bless the bride-beds. Its lightness, its strange simplicity, give them to just as much supernatural dignity as is right and no more. For they are fairies, not gods. But all this the metre itself will all but accomplish, let the actor only yield himself to it. He certainly must not by anything he may do violate the general harmony of the verse.

Oberon's squabble with Titania stands, of course, as counterpart to the lovers' quarrelling. The fairy couple are indeed (and if the play was written for the occasion of a wedding the point is more pertinent) gibbeted as a comically awful warning of what marriage may turn to if jealousy and temper get the upper hand. But, paying due respect to their majesties, and the better to accommodate such distasteful matters in a story that is to end in a triple bridal, they are made merely daintily ridiculous. Titania and Theseus! Oberon and Hippolyta! What childish nonsense! And to make each other miserable, all for the sake of a little Indian boy! Sensible human beings never behave like that – unless they are bewitched.

There may be, then, even such a slight air of travesty about the two, even as the four lovers, being bewitched, will lightly travesty their saner selves. But is Oberon's fairy disposition so strange to us after all? Certainly he is very otuspoken. Without a blush he says,

Thou shalt not from this grove
Till I torment thee for this injury.

A moment later, how the callousness of Demetrius shocks him! No matter, a little magic will put all right. And then, as this goes wrong, a little more magic. For he does not take very long views or pause to consider what may be round the corner, and what he wants he must have done instanter and without question. He has next to see the terrible results of his good intentions, watches in stupefied silence the four poor mortals brought even to tears and to blows. Then he bethinks himself and turns again to his Titania. Even so, he'll not forgive her unless he gets his way. He must taunt her at his pleasure, and she in mild terms beg his patience. But every now and then passion and self-will are lost in a serene self-forgetfulness. For a moment amidst the jarring the beauty of a flower or the thought of the shining moon will absorb him. And always behind his busy inconsequence there dwells the sense —

> But we are spirits of another sort :
> I with the morning's love have oft made sport. . .

All very fairy-like and outlandish! Yet the ironic ear may catch a more familiar echo.

There is hint, though, of a magic wiser than Oberon's, and potent to do us mortals a good turn after all. For hear Demetrius :

> . . . I wot not by what power
> (But by some power it is) my love to Hermia,
> Melted as is the snow, seems to me now
> As the remembrance of an idle gaud,
> Which in my childhood I did dote upon ;
> And all the faith, the virtue of my heart,
> The object, and the pleasure of mine eye,
> Is only Helena.

He wots not by what power, no more do we, no more does Shakespeare. Had he chosen, instead of playing fairy pranks, to write a whole serious play round the question he might still have left it unanswered.

There may be then, we said, a touch of travesty about Oberon. But the word still implies something too clumsy for his fairyhood. It is rather that he is in everything, as one says, just a little too good to be true. He is kinglier than Theseus, more gallant far than Lysander, more despicably jealous than Demetrius, but with a conscienceless ease that makes it all a little unreal. We should smile at him as we are apt to smile at long past romantic visions of ourselves.

So – yet not quite so – with Titania. She is Nature's spoiled darling when things go well; when things go ill with her, all Nature falls into discord. But how she has her way! Flowers and beasts and birds must serve her; and let none of her fairy court be absent for more than a third part of a minute on her errands, or she'll know the reason why. She can do no wrong. What more monstrous than her infatuation for Bottom of the ass's head! What more indelicate than her approaches to him! But Peas-blossom, Cobweb, Moth, Mustardseed and the rest accept the situation without demur. And so must we. Whatever Titania does, she must do so beautifully that it will seem right. While she lavishes her favours on the clumsy fellow, she must almost make us see him with her own enchanted eyes. Not indeed till her silver tongue is silenced and the two fall asleep can we, with the repentant Oberon, realise the horrid truth. Yes, if Titania is ridiculous, we worship her the more for that. See what it means to be a fairy queen.

Upon the reconciliation, though, the touch of travesty must vanish.

> Sound music. Come, my queen, take hands with me,
> And rock the ground whereon these sleepers be.
> Now thou and I are new in amity;
> And will, to-morrow midnight, solemnly,
> Dance in duke Theseus' house triumphantly,
> And bless it to all fair posterity.

And when they come in their dainty majesty, as unheralded as happiness, they must seem to us as simply and naturally beautiful.

The fairy court is certainly no place for idlers. In Titania's service, who could find time to come down off his tiptoes! Peas-blossom and the rest are ever a-hover waiting for commands to blow them hither and thither. Their business is revelry and every other sort of delightful uselessness; and desperately busy they are kept about it

Over hill, over dale,
Through bush, through briar,
Over park, over pale,
Through flood, through fire,
I do wander everywhere,
Swifter than the moon's sphere. . .
I must go seek some dew-drops here,
And hang a pearl in every cowslip's ear.

The cue is given us immediately. How, with our human material, to gain the effect is another matter. Not — we will always hope — by ingenious machinery, gauzes, lighting. Such toys are attractive enough in themselves. Shakespeare, it would seem, fell a victim on occasion to such as he could command; whether a willing or unwilling one, who shall say? But he never turned them to any very remarkable dramatic account; and in this play, quite clearly, he made no allowance for them at all. They are apt to become, then, but an excuse for neglecting the means that are provided.

We do seem to need children, and it is to be supposed that Shakespeare made use of them. Oberon may overtop his subjects, as the king's figure in an ancient painting is drawn to a measure beyond that of ordinary mortals. But bulky fairies simply will not do. What Shakespeare probably did have at his command was a troop of youths excellently trained to speak and sing and move and dance.[14] It is training that is needed; no mere drill through a set of rehearsals, but such training as a dancer gives to his feet and a pianist to his fingers. A producer may manoeuvre his fairies according to judgment and taste, but,

---

[14] The whole question of the employment of children on the stage is a difficult one. The social aspect of it cannot be touched on here. As to the artistic aspect: a self-conscious child is an abomination, and an unself-conscious child romping happily about is apt — even as a beautiful animal will — to make his elder companions look distressingly sophisticated and artificial. Age is a rough measurement in such matters, but one might say that from twelve to fifteen children are susceptible to training and can travel as far in the art as training can take them — which is not very far. Though again, base a complete performance upon training alone and it may be an excellent one, a far more enjoyable one than poor interpretation will produce. At fifteen, one may say, a child becomes capable of interpreting character, crudely or simply enough at first. Thereafter, artistically, he may grow up, or he may merely grow older. (Granville-Barker's note)

to begin with, the exact beauty of their demeanour must be a fitting counterpart to all the beauty of speech the play asks for. The one is, in fact, the proper complement to the other.[15]

Puck accounts himself a fairy, and on the whole we must take his word for it. But he emphasises the fact so boastfully as to suggest that he is at least of another and inferior breed. He is always boasting and swaggering and confidently doing the wrong thing. He bubbles over with incongruous self-importance. He can't go off to pick a flower without remarking that he could – if Oberon should happen to prefer it – girdle the earth for him in forty minutes. Nevertheless, one suspects him to be quite unacquainted with 'the farthest steppe of India.' His range is the Athenian woods (or, it may better be, the county of Warwick). He is a rustic sprite, and his notions of a joke betray it. When Oberon comes 'into residence' he has a tremendous time, showing off his latest tricks, basking – or rather leaping and bounding – in the sun of royal patronage. But, Oberon departed, poor Puck is probably reduced to playing tricks on dairy-maids, has no one but himself to boast to, waits wistfully for the next golden hour to strike. He is of no age, but if he were human he would be young. What his speech may lack in fine tone it makes up for in rhythm. His rougher, rustic touch is in valuable contrast with Oberon and the lovers. He spins the play on its course.

As parts for acting the four lovers have never been highly regarded. As characters they necessarily suffer, we saw, by being sport for Oberon's magic most of the time. But the more the play's interpreting is let depend on the charm of its verse, the better the place, naturally, that the four will find in it, for, between them, they run the compass of its beauty. This apart though, there is some excellent fun in the writing of them; and each has personality enough, and there is contrast enough between all four, to make the weaving in and out of their adventures effective. And the meting of some measure of poetic

---

[15] And this applies, needless to say, with double force to the more important characters in the play; the actors of them must have mastered these things before the characters can come into question at all. (Granville-Barker's note)

justice in this process makes their case the more interesting. Hermia, as vain of her rejected lover – for all she's so off-hand about him! – as she is confident of Lysander, has a rude shock when they both turn from her. Nor does she take this over prettily, as Helena, it must be owned, is a little over-ready to point out to her. And Helena, too, is paid out in her own coin. Mock-modesty is her pose. Then when Lysander and Demetrius compete in adoration for her, she can only believe that they are mocking her too. But Helena is so well-aware of herself that one might almost suspect her of a sense of humour. She sets Demetrius in pursuit of Hermia only to 'enrich her pain'; pursuing him herself, it is hard to believe that she does not enjoy the extreme embarrassment her attentions cause him. This really is a most subtle revenge on Demetrius. And when it comes to argument, – poor thick-headed fellow, he's helpless. At last he reproaches her with immodesty; and that seems a sound stroke. But she retorts that his well-known virtue allows any woman to feel safe with him, a compliment – and surely she need not have put it that way – to which under the circumstances there is no effective reply. And what can make a man more ridiculous than to find himself running away from a woman through a wood in the dark, and to find, moreover, that she can run as fast as he?

This scene, and others, abound in the humour of raillery. They owe their distinction to the musical charm of the verse and the fancy of the images; they are a little too dependent therefore upon nicety of speaking to gain their full effect in any theatre where this is not given pride of place. But, as we have seen, this is true of three quarters of the play. It is true certainly of the pretty duet, with its rhymes and its riddling, between Hermia and Lysander before they lie down to sleep. And Lysander's cool repudiation of her, when the love-juice has worked upon him, must lose half its point unless the slight caricature of the easy charming melodic swing of his former love-making is recognisable; and this implies a delicacy of treatment for both, not easily come by, nor, it must be confessed, likely to appeal to any but sensitive ears. Trained actors ask a trained audience; however, the one earns the other. Clumsier Demetrius, at the first moment of his enchanted waking, caricatures himself, too; out-caricatures Lysander; he pirouettes in jack-boots. No wonder poor Helena cries out:

> . . . I see you all are bent
> To set against me for your merriment.

This scene, thus absurdly begun, gathering complexity with Hermia's arrival, brings the mischief to its full pitch. Oberon, the somewhat astonished author of it, is, we must remember, spectator of the whole, the silently chuckling Robin Goodfellow at his feet. Within the limitation of its method the scene is amazingly well furnished in diversified effect. Long passages of poetry for Helena sustain the play's beauty and romance, — as well as our sentimental interest in the unenchanted fortunes of the four — and they are abruptly followed and set off by the young men's fatuous wrangling. Demetrius, easily outclassed in eloquence, is reduced to the shouted single syllables of

> I say I love thee more than he can do.

The wrangle threatens a scrimmage, with Hermia in the middle of it. The equivoque and criss-cross of the writing here makes fine turmoil. They all fling at each other — as might four smart players at tennis keep the ball flying — till the lead of the scene next passes to Hermia — poor Hermia, brought up against the amazing fact that she and Helena have shifted places and that it is she who is now

> . . . miserable most, to love unlov'd.

Not that she sits down to mourn the matter.

> O me! you juggler! you canker-blossom!
> You thief of love! what, have you come by night,
> And stol'n my love's heart from him?

And — oh, what must Oberon be thinking as he watches! — instead of a gentlemanly fight, we are likely to have a most unladylike one. Another turn of the kaleidoscope. In place of Hermia making peace between the two young men we have Helena sconced between them for safety. And it must be owned that she takes advantage of it:

> Lys. Be not afraid: she shall not harm thee, Helena.
> Dem. No, sir; she shall not, though you take her part.
> Hel. O, when she's angry, she is keen and shrewd:

> She was a vixen when she went to school;
> And, though she be but little, she is fierce.

But fortunately Demetrius and Lysander precipitate the one affair by marching off to fight in seemly solitude, and Helena, her protectors gone, as appropriately precipitates the other by running away.

Then Oberon can vent his anger upon Puck. But the passage that follows abounds in beauty besides. The tangles are unravelling, the fairy blessing impends. Puck, though, may have one more bout of fun.

> Up and down, up and down;
> I will lead them up and down:
> I am fear'd in field and town;
> Goblin, lead them up and down

From here to the scene's end note the variety of the metre, and how well it suits with the quick shifts and turns of the action. This rhythmic incantation, the broken couplets as Puck lures his two victims hither and thither, the steadying or slowing of the verse as they resign themselves to exhaustion and sleep (Lysander the more mellifluously), the gentler beat in the more formal stanzas for Helena and Hermia (sure signs, though, in Hermia's of unabated temper), and, finally, Puck's pleasant little lullaby chant of appeasement.

> On the ground
> Sleep sound:
> I'll apply
> To your eye,
> Gentle lover, remedy.
> When thou wak'st,
> Thou tak'st
> True delight
> In the sight
> Of thy former lady's eye:
> And the country proverb known,
> That every man should take his own,
> In your waking shall be shown:
> Jack shall have Jill;
> Nought shall go ill;

The man shall have his mare again, and all shall be well.

No one, understanding the plain meaning of English and having any ear at all, can possibly go wrong over the speaking of that. It is as surely set to its own essential music as if it were barred and scored.

Theseus and Hippolyta together form the play's centre of gravity. The position in its very nature must forbid overmuch activity, but of such as there is, he certainly takes the hero's share.[16] He is not left quite a lay figure, however. To the conventional furnishings of a romantic-heroic part Shakespeare adds a kindly humour and some mellowness of wisdom, the liker a true hero's as it is carried lightly. His famous peroration upon the lunatic, the lover and the poet might merely serve to count him as one of them. But the less quoted snub to that snobbish Lord Chamberlain, Philostrate (and to Hippolyta also, one fears must be added; for with her wedding she seems to shed the last traces of Amazon and to turn Athenian – or Elizabethan – fine lady, top to toe) is more characteristic and, in its place, dramatically far more effective.

> Where I have come, great clerks have purposed
> To greet me with premeditated welcomes;
> Where I have seen them shiver and look pale,
> Make periods in the midst of sentences,
> Throttle their practis'd accent in their fears,
> And, in conclusion, dumbly have broke off,
> Not paying me a welcome. Trust me, sweet,
> Out of this silence yet I pick'd a welcome;
> And in the modesty of fearful duty
> I read as much as from the rattling tongue
> Of saucy and audacious eloquence.
> Love, therefore, and tongue-tied simplicity
> In least speak most, to my capacity.

This is kingly.

---

[16] One of those dangerous moments, that are dear to the heart of the actor as providing (some recompense!) more amusement for him than the audience, is to be found – and circumvented – when in the first scene Theseus turns to the apparently long-forgotten Hippolyta with 'What cheer, my love.' It is open to the poor lady to revenge herself soundly upon Shakespeare by responding with a meaning smile. Thus does one enliven dull rehearsals. (Granville-Barker's note)

And if the play really was written for a wedding feast and was first played to brides, bridegrooms and guests, then the dovetailing of the interlude into the play and the making its audience a mirror and echo of the actual audience becomes a delightful dramatic device. Of this, we can, of course, re-capture little or nothing of the effect; and the fairy benediction, once so charged with meaning, becomes, in the casual theatre, a matter of pleasant-sounding verse, hardly more.[17]

Shakespeare, it is to be feared, played somewhat false by the clowns. A clown is a rustic fellow, a townsman will call him a comic fellow. There is ample scope here for observant humour; so there is in the countryman's opinion of the townsman, could he make it articulate. Shakespeare knew enough of both town and country to play the honest broker between them. With Quince, Bottom and the rest he begins fairly enough. What could be more delightfully observant than their first assembly, than the rehearsal in the wood – or, indeed, than the mourning for Bottom's defection, or even than the beginning of the interlude itself? But in the theatre as he found it, there was the other sort of clown to be considered, the clown who played the clown; and, more often – as his antics have taught us now-a-days to express it – clowned the clown. And to the chief of these fell the character of Bottom. Therefore while it is partly the best thing in the play, it is, perhaps, partly the worst. Nor will it do to attribute its lapses (as we can, for instance, with the Fool in *King Lear*) to an actor speaking more than was set down for him – and having it set down. They are not, on the whole, of that robust and inconsiderate foolishness which marks the hail-fellow humour of the popular comedian. It is rather as if Shakespeare had felt upon this occasion that his actor would not be content without some dollops of the usual non-sense and had indifferently provided a few, leaving him to en-

---

[17] Can we detect, too, Shakespeare's own mock apology for the imperfections of his work, put into the mouth of Theseus? Did Shakespeare, by any remote chance, play the part himself? It was in his line, according to tradition, and, if so, the joke would have been a good one indeed.

Marry, if he that writ it, had play'd Pyramus, and hanged himself
in Thisbe's garter, it would have been a fine tragedy.
(Granville-Barker's note)

rich them if he could — and doubtless he did! We have, in fact, now Bottom the Weaver and, again, Bottom the buffoon. We know, of course, that Shakespeare had fault to find with the comic actors of his day, though we may fairly weigh the kindlier reference to the clown in *Twelfth Night* against the more commonly quoted passage from *Hamlet*. But there is evidence from all sides that playwrights and judicious spectators both began to find the clowns a nuisance. There had begun, in fact, that never-ending battle of the drama against its actors — though many an actor, no doubt, then as now, was valiantly on the drama's side. One difficulty was that the Clown, the 'all-licens'd Fool,' had, so to speak, occupied the ground first, claiming a traditional right to his place there. His licence, expiring at Court, found yet fuller scope in the theatre. Not that Shakespeare had any fundamental grudge against him. In his legitimate motley, agile, a sweet singer, skilled on the pipe and tabor, he is given delightful employment in play after play. The difficulty would arise when comic *character* had to be interpreted. And this is a fundamental difficulty, and it remains to this day; it cannot perhaps ever be overcome. For your 'born comedian,' your 'funny man' is only funny if he may be himself — exaggeratedly and ridiculously himself. If he lets that self be absorbed in an alien character, he is lost in every sense. He cannot, indeed, so yield himself, and a forced attempt to leaves him cramped and unhappy. It is unreasonable to complain. His art, of its sort, is a perfectly legitimate one. But if a dramatist wants to make full use of it, he must leave scope for the bubbling, irresponsible native humour and for the doing and even speaking of much more than it will be possible to set down. This art, though, for all the likeness, is not the art of the interpretative actor. And it is when Shakespeare provides a part such as Bottom the Weaver, which calls for interpretation, yet both leaves and does not leave scope for sheer funniment, yields it half-heartedly, yields it grudgingly, that trouble arises. Whether on this occasion Master Shakespeare lost his habitual good temper with Master William Kempe for playing the fool too outrageously, whether, as is more likely, Master Kempe was aggrieved to find his part (if he did play it) rather thin where there should have been most 'fat' in it, or whether this was not, as it happened, one of the provocations to the penning of that passage in *Hamlet*, it is useless to speculate. Our dilemma remains.[18]

We have the Bottom of the first two scenes, the rustic Roscius among his fellow rustics. He is not fooling; there is not a smile on his face, nor a twinkle in his eye. He faces his responsibilities – and everyone else's – with solid seriousness. Like a later amateur of legend, could he have been cast for Othello, he would have blacked himself all over. How did he scape – we fear the Duke was thrifty, and he did – that sixpence a day for life? This is, from the legitimate, the observantly humorous actor's point of view, the real thing, and he will know how to treat it. The passages with Titania are well enough; if neither Shakespeare nor any actor can make more of them it is mainly the fault of the ass-head with which both are burdened. But the waking from the dream is the thinnest and emptiest of stuff. Here, if the actor cannot somehow contrive to do more than the author has done, his audience must only wish that he could. And, as far as Bottom is concerned, the return to his sorrowing fellows is no better. Then, in the interlude itself, Shakespeare seems to say, after some hesitation, after extracting some genuine comedy from good Quince's tragedy, 'Oh, well, here you are' –

> Now am I dead,
> Now am I fled;
> My soul is in the sky.

This and more like it is not funny in the sense that the stuttering of the prologue, the innocence of Wall and Lion, Bottom's own aside to Theseus, are funny. It comes decidedly amiss. It is not the sort of thing that simpleness and duty tenders – and Shakespeare knew that well enough. Did he throw this bit of 'fat' to his comedian as a bone to a dog, that he, in turn, might

[18] Is no combination of the two sorts of comedy possible? This may well have been Shakespeare's own exasperated question. Yes, every now and then, a peculiarly sympathetic and sensitive, a two-sided talent will be an exception to the rule. Did Shakespeare find, or think he had found, such a one to play the Fool in *King Lear*? 'Think' must be added; for whence came a few of those lines that smear the play? (Granville-Barker's note)

throw it to the audience? He allots to his mock audience some specimens of the pretentious and even sillier jokes with which, presumably, such young sparks were wont to interrupt his own plays. Was that his sly revenge upon them for their greedy gobbling of the husks of his art as well as the good grain? Or – and it is likelier – did he do it all with a divine carelessness; as he would ever, it seems, make the most of a scene that came happily to life under his hand, let another hang limp if it wouldn't, and impenitently bolster up a third with mechanical foolery if the need were?

This, at least, is the case for the prosecution, Bottom in the dock. On all counts doubtless a defence can be set up. Bottom is ineffective when he awakes because he is still distraught with the enchantment. His jokes when he rejoins the despairing company are flavourless, because he is in haste and the interlude is impending. And some actual instance of such Arcadian art-lessness as 'Now am I dead' can quite possibly be brought into evidence. This last, though, would be a poor aesthetic plea. And what cannot be argued away is the fact that the real fun of Bottom lies in the one set of scenes and not in the other.

To face our dilemma: when we stage the play, which sort of a clown is Bottom to be? Down to Charles Lamb and Hazlitt's day (and considerably later, though not with such credit) the tradition of the droll survived, and mummery and even gagging was allowable. But to-day we approach our Shakespeare hieratically, and the droll has been banished to the music-hall. It is in some ways a pity. Too solemn a reverence needs an antidote. But recall him and he would return an intimidated man, and nothing is duller than half-hearted foolery. Better then, at any rate where Bottom is concerned, give value to the part of him which Shakespeare, by every sign, whole-heartedly liked writing – we shall get good value from it – and let the rest go for what it may still prove worth.

For the best of him, the simplest of him, is so irresistibly good.

> An I may hide my face, let me play Thisby too.
> I'll speak in a monstrous little voice . . .

He is so earnest, so confident, so resolved on success, so willing to bear the burden of it; and after all who should, who can, but he? But Quince, the ever-tactful, fends him off; then hurries – does he? – through his giving out the rest of the parts for fear lest yet another should strike Bottom's fancy, till with relief he can turn from Snug the joiner with

> I hope here is a play fitted.

If Snug could but have left well alone! Untimely diffidence!

> Have you the lion's part written? pray you, if it be give it me, for I am slow of study.
>
> You may do it extempore, for it is nothing but roaring.

Quince has a pretty wit, a dry and academic wit. Surely he is the author of the interlude. Is he not ready to turn out a prologue in eight and six. But is this a time for trifling? Bottom intervenes:

> Let me play the lion too: I will roar that I will do any man's heart good to hear me; I will roar that I will make the Duke say, 'Let him roar again, let him roar again.'

Quince returns to diplomacy, a twinkle in his eye.

> An you should do it too terribly you would fright the duchess and the ladies, that they would shriek; and that were enough to hang us all.

This tells – on the rest!

> That would hang us, every mother's son.

And who so conscious as Bottom of the risks they would run without him?

> I grant you, friends, if you should fright the ladies out of their wits, they would have no more discretion but to hang us: but I will aggravate my voice so, that I will roar you as gently as any sucking dove; I will roar you an 'twere any nightingale.

Whereat poor Quince loses his temper – and very nearly his leading actor too. Flattery may still save the situation; why ever be sparing of it?

> You can play no part but Pyramus: for Pyramus is a sweet faced man; a proper man, as one shall see in a summer's day; a most lovely, gentleman-like man; therefore you must needs play Pyramus.
> Well, I will undertake it.

After which turn of magnanimity they are all quite content to listen to a list of his fancies in that important matter of the beard he must wear.

This and the like of it is no foolery, but what better fun do we need? The kindly, crotchety, whimsical Quince, the modest Flute, the meek Snug, cautious Snout, amenable Starveling, with lordly Bottom to lead them! Sweet bully Bottom, the best wit of any handicraft man in Athens, with the best person, and a very paramour for a sweet voice! He can teach the Duke himself a thing or two about the theatre and how to behave there — and, being in his element, does!

If these are clowns, it is not in any motley sense. Rather they are the wholesomely humorously human foundation, without which the airy poetic structure of the play might well be too weak to stand.

Variants in The Text

FOR a standard text I have taken that of the Oxford Shakespeare, edited by W. J. Craig, 1919. I note below only some few readings that I venture to prefer, or that invite comment. And for record of other readings I am in debt, as who is not? to Furness. In a play's acting, when all depends on hearing and immediate understanding, one is tempted to abide — if there is legitimate doubt — by the most effective phrase. I think it a temptation that may, more often than not, be yielded to.

Omit all scene-divisions and descriptions, and upon the question of division into acts see the body of the preface.

Act I, Sc. i, 69. 'Whe'r.' F1 has 'Whether,' and I see no practical reason to alter spelling or pronunciation.

81. 'whose unwished yoke.' The 'to whose' of F2, 3, 4 may be needless, but for us it is convenient, and 'unwish'd' comes as constantly as 'unwished.'

143. 'momentary.' Q may be right, but – again F1's 'momentary' does suit us better to-day.

182. 'your fair.' Yet again I incline to the 'you fair' of F1.

Scene ii, 25. 'gallantly.' Now, on the contrary, I find in the 'gallant' of Q a flavour that this lacks.

30. As the 'rest yet' of Q and F1 must be altered, we may as well have 'rest. Yet . . .' for this is what the speaking really demands.

56. 'Thisne, Thisne.' One is tempted by the reading which would make this mean (practically) 'thusly, thusly,' if only the point could be made verbally good. This apart, it must stand for Pyramus's pet name for his lady-love.

86. 'as' read 'an.'

115. 'hold,' omit comma.

Act II, Sc. i, 3, 5. 'thorough.' Here again F1 has helped us to 'through,' and I see no reason to refuse the help.

7. 'Moone's.' F1 has 'moons,' the omission of the apostrophe being, of course, a small matter. It does no real harm to the rhythm.

42. 'Fairy, thou speak'st aright.' Neither Q nor F has 'Fairy,' and there is no valid excuse for the interpolation.

54. F1 'tailor.' Furness's collection of notes and his own apt comment may be read for instruction and entertainment both. But when it comes to speaking the word they avail nothing.

106. 'thorough.' Here again F1 has 'through.'

But here it does mar the rhythm, and for that reason, and that only, I prefer this Q reading. Or shall one be consistent, as, in this scene, Q is and F is? I should suppose that in their use and pronunciation of the variations upon 'through' and 'thorough' the Elizabethans were neither constant nor consistent. We have reached some constancy without much consistency. As far as the playing of Shakespeare is concerned, this is, of course, part of a larger question.

192. 'wood within this wood.' If the first should be 'wôd,' i.e. enraged, though the meaning may no longer be clear, the very sound can be made to carry something of it. But 'wood' makes poor sense, if any.

220. 'privilege: for that.' This is authoritative; but I follow the many editors who place the stop at the end of the line.

242. *Exit Demetrius.* This is not marked in either Q or F1. It is open to a producer to place it after line 240, Helena speaking the next two lines to herself, Demetrius stealing off unseen while she does so; to leave it where it is, — which allows her a loud apostrophe to the just vanished gentleman; or to place it after line 244, which implies that, having endured as much as he could, he breaks suddenly away. I prefer either 1 or 3 to 2.

249. 'whereon.' Read 'where,' according to Q and F1 both.

Scene ii, 104. 'shows art.' I rather prefer 'shows her art,' though I would not go to the stake for it.

Act III, Sc. i, 81. *Enter Puck, behind.* Puck's entry after line 57, for which there is equally good authority (F1), may well be more effective.

Scene ii, 81. 'whe'r,' read 'whether.'

201. 'is it all forgot.' No need, I think, to alter F1's 'is all forgot.'

204. 'neelds.' Again F1 has 'needles,' and it can be made so nearly a monosyllable in pronunciation that I see no good reason to alter it.

257. 'No, no, he'll . . .' This given to Demetrius does not make dramatic sense. Given to Hermia it does. As she says it, she presumably flings her arms round Lysander to protect him.

265. 'Do you not jest.' Every now and then one wishes for italics. The 'not' must be strongly emphasised.

344. I suppose there is nothing to do but to admit this line of Hermia's from Q. But it is lame, impotent and uncharacteristic. One would think that it covers the cutting out of something more considerable, and that later (when the copy for F1 was in the making) it seemed to someone that no line at all was better than this. A producer might well try to provide for Hermia's exit without it.

Act IV, Scene i. Upon the questions of Oberon's entrance and the omission of the 'rurall musicke,' see the body of the preface.

41. 'thence.' The interpolation is more allowable than most.

89–91. The music, which is still or soft music, should only begin upon Oberon's command.

96. 'prosperity.' I prefer the 'posterity' of F1.

199. 'Are you sure that we are yet awake?' I much prefer to follow F1 and omit this. It spoils both the following sentences and the effect of (204) 'Why then, we are awake.'

226. 'at her death.' Surely Theobald is right and it should be 'after death.'

Scene ii, 13–14. One is strongly tempted to a redistribution here: either to give the whole of Quince's line to Snout; or (better) to give the last half of it to anyone but Quince, and, possibly, to allot him Flute's speech that follows.

This is very arbitrary and cannot wholly be justified, for Quince has talked about disfiguring or presenting Wall. Nevertheless one is tempted. I think it is Flute putting Quince right that seems the really unlikely thing, though he might be bold enough to correct Snout.

Act v, Sc. i, 10. An unnecessary comma has crept in after 'That is.'

38–58. The ascriptions of F1 are very confusing here. In practice there is nothing to be said for depriving Philostrate of speeches. But Lysander's reading of the brief, leaving Theseus the comments only, might be worth trying.

Scene ii, 128. 'as in dumb show.' I am not quite sure what Mr Craig means by this. I think it is only a formal procession of the characters.

331. 'moans.' One fears it should be 'means'; but here is an instance of the temptation in a slighly more effective phrase.

352. 'stabs herself.' May we not venture (see the note in Furness's Variorum) to add 'with the scabbard.' Bottom presumably is lying on the sword.

Scene iii, 49–50. These two lines should, I feel sure, be transposed.

'Preface to A MIDSUMMER NIGHT'S DREAM,'
London, Ernest Benn Ltd., 1924 pp. ix–lii.
(The fourth volume of *The Players' Shakespeare*.)

From *Henry V* to *Hamlet*

I WANT to speak of what seems to me to have been the crucial period of Shakespeare's development as a dramatist, and to glance at what prompted the crisis and what resulted from it. And if I must seem dogmatic, it is not that I am in love with my dogma, or feel dogmatic at all, but merely that in spending an hour upon a controversial subject one must save time. I shall speak of him simply as a dramatist, and primarily as an Elizabethan dramatist; a view too long ignored, though now returning to favour. In fact for an ideal standpoint I would throw myself and you back, if I could, by not quite three hundred years, to be listeners to such a talk as I imagine might have had place – let us say about 1635, at the Pegasus Inn in Cheapside, and at supper time, between three playgoers returned from some performance at the Blackfriars; not of one of Shakespeare's plays, but of the latest Massinger or Shirley.

The chill shadow of Puritanism was already falling, and within seven years the theatres were to be closed. It was the time of the decadence of Elizabethan drama; though that, no doubt, was a question of contemporary dispute. I will imagine our three playgoers disputing it. Let one of them be elderly, and the two others young; one of these two an enthusiast, and the other – as common a type – a great frequenter of theatres and a greater despiser of them. After a while the elder might drift – if the supper and the wine and the company were generous I feel sure he *would* drift – into reminiscence of the better time 'when you young blades were in your cradles,' when Shakespeare and Burbage were the men. It is to such a point of

view of Shakespeare's art that I wish I could lead you this after-
noon. For from it we could still see him as the topical wit, and
he was that; as the successor to Kyd and Marlowe, in a perspec-
tive which would give us the contemporary value of that heri-
tage; as the popular playwright and the provider of effective
parts for Burbage, Heminge, Phillips, Field, Pope, and the rest;
for he was this too, and upon this must have hung much of his
contemporary reputation. Finally, I suspect, we should have to
consider him as the dramatist who – his head turned by too
much success, maybe – tried to do more with the theatre than
the theatre's nature allowed, and, for all his reputation, failed.
The youngest of the trio, our contemptuous playgoer would I feel
sure, urge this very smartly. (Had he lately spent 20s., perhaps,
upon a nice new copy of the second folio? A second-hand copy
of the first would have been a better investment for the future.)

'*Hamlet*? Yes, interesting; but I'd sooner read than see it.
Can it be a good play then? *Macbeth,* with its elliptical obscuri-
ties of language – do you call that poetry? *King Lear,* with its
verbal thundering and lightning, and the whole thing as
inchoate as the thunder-storm – is this sort of stuff suitable to a
theatre?'

In which last objection, of course, most modern critics join;
but they are apt to blame the theatre and not Shakespeare for it.
We should perhaps have heard his earlier work preferred to his
later. Did he, after all, ever do anything more delightful than
Love's Labour's Lost and *Richard II*? Or his latest liked better
than all; the pastoral scenes in *The Winter's Tale* and *The
Tempest.* And our young and contemptuous playgoer – who
had in prospect, shall we suppose, a career of acrid success in
the Long Parliament till Cromwell should grow sick of his
sophistries – would finally protest that the only play he un-
reservedly admired was *Troilus and Cressida.* At last the elder
man, capturing the talk, would tell them what he thought really
happened to Shakespeare, the popular playwright, at the crux
of his career.

'Let me remember. When was it I first saw *Julius Caesar*?
About 1600. Yes, thirty-five years ago. . . .'

It is his discourse which, with unavoidable differences, I will
try to make mine.

In 1599 Shakespeare produced *Henry V*. He was at a height of success and popularity. He had never looked back since Marlowe died and left him, so to speak, the sceptre of heroic blank verse as a legacy. In *Henry V* he is wielding that sceptre — incomparably and with a difference — but it is that same sceptre still. The play was, no doubt, a contemporary success. But it bears signs, like many successes, of having brought its writer to a 'dead end.' And, standing at Shakespeare's side at that moment (I do not suggest he did anything of the sort himself), one might pertinently have asked: 'In what has the vitality of your work really lain?'

The answer must involve a glance at the development of the whole Elizabethan theatre up to this time. Roughly speaking this is what has been happening. Within the rather more than twenty years since the building of James Burbage's famous theatre — *The* Theatre — these stageplayers' pranks have become in some opinions a pleasing and an almost respectable calling, out of which, that is to say, people are beginning to make reputation and money. There has developed a school — several schools — of playwrights. There has necessarily developed also a school of actors. This last phenomenon was possibly the more noticeable one to the Elizabethans, though it is in restrospect, of course, the less obvious to us. But let us look into it a little. What players did the earlier dramatists find to draw upon? Foremost in popularity with the public were the clowns. But from the dramatist's point of view they were not very satisfactory actors. Their skill lay in dancing and singing and improvisation; the shackles of set dialogue, as we know, they as often broke as wore. More important recruits for the poetic need of the plays would be the boys — now growing and grown to be men — the child actors trained by Farrant and his like in such choir schools as St Paul's. Delicate, charming, scholarly speakers, we may be sure. Translate their acting at Court or the Blackfriars into the terms of the singing in a good Cathedral choir to-day, and you have approximately the aesthetic effect they made. But they would find a very different audience in the open public theatres, to which the whole unruly town might come. Put this in political terms; it would be the difference between a debate in the House of Lords and an 'Irish' night in Parnell's day in the Commons. Then there would be the barn-stormers, the actors of all work, who had, with one qualification or another, found a place in this or that company of 'Lords' men.'

We must consider, then, the development of the drama from 1580 to 1600 from the point of view (among others) of its interpretation; and this in the light of the combination of skilled youth and glorified barn-storming – glorified by the gifts and demands of the young poet-dramatists, of Marlowe and Shakespeare in particular. It was surely this new art of emotional acting which gave the drama its sudden hold on the people. The older plays had not provided for anything like this. If we ask what sort of acting it was that people found so stirring, there are parallels to-day, though the nearest are not in the theatre. Go to a revivalist meeting in Wales – or, if you prefer, go to the Opera. Elizabethan music did not attempt the frontal assault on our emotions that much modern music does; modern opera, in particular. But orotund drama was a rough equivalent. And if anyone recollects, some twenty-five years ago at Covent Garden, Caruso's finish to the first act of *Pagliacci,* I think they can estimate the sort of effect created by Alleyn and (while he emulated him) Burbage on the Elizabethan stage. Much else, however, had gone to the making of the complete art of the theatre as it existed in 1600. Skill in high comedy and the development out of clowning of what we now call 'character' acting. Externally, richer resources for properties and costume; a fair touch of pageantry. But the heroes of the public as of the plays were Burbage and Alleyn and their peers, for they gave their audience music and poetry and popular oratory in one.[1]

Now let us see what Shakespeare's characteristic contributions to the theatre had been. There were the obvious ones; and some not yet perhaps quite so obvious. For there were two sides to Shakespeare the playwright, as there are to most artists, and to most men brought into relations with the public and its

---

[1] It is likely, I think, that Alleyn, conquering the town with Tamburlaine, set a high standard of rhetorical acting, and more than possible that he never did anything better, or very different. Burbage, on the other hand, though he may have begun on these lines, must have developd his art out of all knowledge in subtlety and resource by the time he came to play Hamlet, Othello, and Lear. (Granville-Barker's note, 1932)

appetite (which flatterers call its taste). There was the complaisant side and the daemonic side. His audience demanded exciting stories. He was no great hand at inventing a story, but he borrowed the best. They asked for heroic verse. He could do this with any one, and he did. I always fancy that the immoderate length of *Richard III* is due to the sheer exuberance of the young man put on his mettle to claim the inheritance of the dead Marlowe's mighty line. Euphuism had its vogue still. He could play upon that pipe too very prettily; and *Love's Labour's Lost* is as much homage as satire. But from the very beginning, signs of the daemonic Shakespeare can be seen, the genius bent on having his own way; of the Shakespeare to whom the idea is more than the thing, who cares much for character and little for plot, who cannot indeed touch the stagiest figure of fun without treating it as a human being and giving it life, whether it suits Shakespeare the popular play-provider to do so or not. And sometimes it doesn't. Life in the theatre will play the devil with artifice.

Look into *Love's Labour's Lost*. We laugh the play through at the ridiculous Armado; no mockery, not the crudest sort of banter is spared him. But at the end, with one touch of queer, pathetic, dignity, Shakespeare and he make the fine gentlemen of the play, who are mirrors of the fine gentlemen in the audience, look pretty small. Consider Sir Nathaniel the country curate. The late Mr W. S. Penley in *The Private Secretary*[2] was no greater scandal to the dignity of the Church (though Mr Penley also knew too much about comedy not always to keep a little dignity in hand) than is Sir Nathaniel attempting to enact Alexander the Great. But, when he has been laughed off the mimic stage, hear Costard's apology for him to the smart London ladies and gentlemen, his mimic audience:

> There, an't shall please you; a foolish mild man; an honest man look you, and soon dashed! He is a marvellous good neighbour, faith, and a very good bowler; but for Alisander – alas, you see how 'tis, a little o'erparted.

---

[2] An 1883 adaptation of a comedy by Von Moser by the actor Sir Charles Hawtrey (1858–1923, Knighted 1922). Penley (1842–1912) acted the title role innumerable times.

That does not belong to the plot or the mere fun-making scheme. Nor is it a thing you learn to do by following any fashion or going to any school of play-writing, to-day's or yesterday's. But here already, in 1591, his age twenty-five, is the true Shakespeare having his way. Fifty words (not so many) turn Sir Nathaniel the Curate (and Costard too) from a stage puppet to a human being, and send you away from the theatre, not only knowing the man, having, as we say, 'an idea' of the man, but liking him even while you laugh at him, and feeling, moreover, a little kindlier towards the next man you meet in the street who reminds you of him. *This* is the Shakespeare who was finally to people, not his little theatre only, but the whole intellectual world for the next three hundred years with figures of his imagining.

This is the Shakespeare that turns the Romeo of Act I into the Romeo of Act V, and the Mercutio of the Queen Mab speech (charming stuff though it be) into the Mercutio of

> No! 'tis not so deep as a well, nor so wide as a church door; but 'tis enough, 'twill serve. . . .

It is the Shakespeare who recklessly lodged that dynamic human figure of Shylock within the preposterous fairy tale of *The Merchant of Venice,* the Shakespeare who triumphantly made the Falstaff of the speech on Honour and of the scenes of *Henry IV, Part II* out of the old pickpurse of Gadshill (strange that a later inhabitant of Gadshill should have done much the same sort of thing two and a half centuries later with his *Pickwick*). If in fact we are to look for the informing thing, the vital quality in Shakespeare's developing art, it will lie not in the weaving and unravelling of plots, but in some spirit behind the plot, by which it seems to move of itself; and not so much in the writing of great dramatic poetry even, as in this growing power to project character in action.

Now if emotional rhetoric was a new thing to the Elizabethan theatre, this last thing – done as he was doing it – was yet a newer. To-day we can distinguish him in the first stage of his career passing from sketches to full length figures, from the play and the part that is half convention and half a living thing (read the entire Juliet; not the Juliet as commonly cut for performance) to the thing that abounds in its own life from first to last. It was not such an easy journey to make; for Shakespeare the daemonic genius had always to strike some sort of a bargain with Shakespeare the popular playwright, who would be content with the finish of *The Taming of the Shrew* or the last Act of *The Two Gentlemen of Verona*. But truly the bolder spirit was justified by success, and went from success to success, from Richard III to Richard II, from Shylock to Falstaff, from Mercutio to Hotspur, from Romeo to Prince Hal.

This, you may protest, is merely to say that he was learning how to write good plays. For is not the chief test of a good play that its characters will come vividly to life when it is acted? It is easier, as we shall see, to call this a truism than to admit all that its truth must imply. Make such a comparison, however, between Shakespeare and his contemporaries; set, for instance, Marlowe's Edward II by his Richard II's side, and see if here is not the essential difference between them. Then look closer to where the actual detailed differences lie. How does this vitality manifest itself? Did we not mark it rightly in that little speech of Costard's in *Love's Labour's Lost*? Is not Shakespeare's progress as a playwright very much to be measured by the increase of those suddenly illuminating things that seem to light up not merely the one dramatic moment, but the whole nature of a man, sometimes even the very background of his life? By such things as Prince Hal's famous apostrophe to Falstaff, shamming dead:

> Poor Jack, farewell,
> I could have better spared a better man.

— As Mr Justice Shallow's

> Barren, barren, barren; beggars all, beggars all, Sir John. Marry, good air!

— such as the hostess's tale of Falstaff's death:

> . . . I knew there was but one way; for his nose was as sharp as a pen, and a' babbled of green fields.

— and old drink-sodden Bardolph's

> Would I were with him, wheresome'er he is, either in heaven or in hell.

Are such things trifles? They are immortal trifles. They should not be torn from their context, and their true context is the acted scene. But are they not the things that give this peculiar quality of life to the plays? And is it not the ever greater abundance of this quality which marks his approach to the mastery of his art?

Shakespeare was learning too, in these years, to adapt the chief convention of his medium – the convention of rhetorical verse – to his own needs. He had also, it is true, the directer one of prose; and he could make a magnificent music of that when he chose. Falstaff certainly lacks nothing of force or fire by being freed from the bonds of metre.

> If sack and sugar be a fault, God help the wicked. If to be old and merry be a sin, then many an old host that I know is damned; if to be fat be to be hated, then Pharaoh's lean kine are to be loved. No, my good lord, banish Peto, banish Bardolph, banish Poins; but for sweet Jack Falstaff, kind Jack Falstaff, true Jack Falstaff, valiant Jack Falstaff, and therefore more valiant being as he is, old Jack Falstaff, banish not him thy Harry's company: banish not him thy Harry's company: banish plump Jack, and banish all the world.

But compare Romeo and Richard II with Hotspur and Prince Hal. Hotspur is set almost entirely within the convention of verse; but how little conventionalised phrasing there is in it. And Prince Hal's turns from prose to verse, with the turns of his character, are made with excellent ease. And the caricature of the convention in Pistol is worth remark.

Shakespeare is working, as most artists will, towards making his medium perfectly malleable, and is developing technical resource which defeats mere technical criticism. He was ever a forthright worker; he would precipitate himself into tight places, and then with extraordinary daring and agility be out of them (think of the time-problem in *Othello,* and of the manoeuvring of the sub-plot in *King Lear*). He came to possess, indeed, that combination of judgement and instinct which, serving another end, made the deeds of our young airmen in the War a marvel that their elders by reason alone could neither rival nor explain. And, to further the comparison, Shakespeare was working in the youth of an art, to which such freedom is more allowable. Let us not suppose, though, that, for all their seemingly slap-dash ways, these Elizabethan dramatists would not be concerned with the technique of their craft. They had not developed its vocabulary. They did not write books, or have to listen to lectures on the subject; though one may suspect that rare Ben Jonson thumped the tables of the Mermaid pretty hard to this purpose. But by an older and better dispensation the little group of comrades and rivals would bandy sharp personal criticism upon work in the doing with the religious fervour which properly belongs to a living art.

Somewhat thus, then, Shakespeare stood towards the theatre when he set out upon the writing of *Henry V*. What is it, in this play, which disappoints us – which, as I believe, disappointed him – and marks it as the dangerpoint of his career?

From now on I will but assemble before you, as a counsel might, the facts that I think sustain my view of this artistic crisis through which Shakespeare passed. I do not, of course, attach equal importance to them all. Nor do I pretend that, the truth of one admitted, the truth of another must follow. For, however else Shakespeare's genius worked, it was not upon logical lines, and to put anything about it to that test is almost certainly to be misled.

Well, here he is, an acknowledged master of his craft and in the full flush of success, setting out to write a fine play, a spacious play, with England as its subject, no less a thing. He is now to crown the achievement of the earlier histories and, above all, of the last two, in which he had so 'found himself.' He is to bring that popular favourite Prince Hal to a worthy completion; and to this obligation – though against his formal promise to the public – he sacrifices Falstaff. It is easy to see why. Could Falstaff reform and be brought back into the company of the reformed Henry? No. Once before Shakespeare has hinted to us that the fat knight, if he grow great shall grow less, purge, leave sack, and live cleanly. But not a bit of it. *Henry IV, Part II,* when it came, found him more incorrigible than ever. On the other hand, had Falstaff made his unauthorised way to France, how could Henry's new dignity suffer the old ruffian's ironic comments on it? He had run away with his creator once : better not risk it. So to his now unimpeachable hero Shakespeare has to sacrifice his greatest, his liveliest creation so far. Does the hero reward him? No one could say that Henry is ill-drawn or uninteresting. But, when it comes to the point, there seems to be very little that is dramatically interesting for him to do. Here is a play of action, and here is the perfect man of action. Yet all the while Shakespeare is apologising – and directly apologising – for not being able to make the action effective. Will the audience, for heaven's sake, help him out? One need not attach too much importance to the formal modesty of the prologue.

> O pardon! Since a crooked figure may
> Attest in little place a million,
> And let us, ciphers to this great accompt,
> On your imaginary forces work.

This might be merely the plea of privilege that every playwright, ancient and modern, must tacitly make. But when we find the apology repeated and repeated again, and before Act V most emphatically of all; when we find there the prayer to his audience

> . . . to admit the excuse
> Of time, of numbers, and due course of things
> Which cannot in their huge and proper life
> Be here presented –

does it not sound a more than formal confession, and as if Shakespeare had distressfully realised that he had asked his theatre – mistakenly; because it must be mistakenly – for what it could not accomplish?

Turn now to Henry himself. When do we come closest to him? Not surely in the typical moments of the man of action, in

> Once more unto the breach, dear friends, once more . . .

and upon like occasions. But in the night before Agincourt, when, on the edge of likely disaster, he goes out solitary into the dark and searches his own soul. This is, of course, no new turn to the character. Prince Hal at his wildest has never been a figure of mere fun and bombast. Remember the scenes with his father and with Hotspur. Still, soul-searching is – if one may use such a phrase of Majesty – not his long suit; and the passage, fine as it is, has the sound of a set piece. It is rhetoric rather than revelation.

In the later speech to Westmoreland:

> We few, we happy few, we band of brothers . . .

Henry, set among his fellows, is more himself. But Shakespeare makes practically no further attempt to show us the inner mind of the man. The Henry of the rest of Act IV is the Henry of the play's beginning. While, since for Act V some new aspect of the hero really must be found, we are landed with a jerk (nothing in the character has prepared us for it) into a rollicking love scene. And this well-carpentered piece of work is finished. I daresay it was a success, and the Shakespeare who lived to please and had to please to live, may have been content with it. But the other, the daring, the creative Shakespeare, who had now known what it was to have Shylock, Mercutio, Hotspur, and Falstaff come to life, and abound in unruly life, under his hands – was he satisfied? No doubt he could have put up as good a defence as many of his editors have obliged him with both for hero and play, for its epic quality and patriotic purpose. Though had he read in the preface to the admirable Arden edition that—

> Conscientious, brave, just, capable and tenacious, Henry stands before us the embodiment of worldly success, and as such he is entitled to our unreserved admiration . . .

I think he would have smiled wryly. For he was not the poet to find patriotism an excuse for the making of fine phrases. And he knew well enough that neither in the theatre nor in real life is it these 'embodiments of wordly success' that we carry closest in our hearts, or even care to spend an evening with.

No, he had set himself this task, and he carried it through conscientiously and with the credit which is sound workmanship's due. But I detect disappointment with his hero, and – not quite fancifully, I believe – a deeper disillusion with his art.

K

The 'daemonic' Shakespeare, then, was only a lesson to the good. But it was a valuable lesson. He had learnt that for presenting the external pageantry of great events his theatre was no better than a puppet-show; and that though the art of drama might be the art of presenting men in action, your successful man of action did not necessarily make the most interesting of heroes. For behind the action, be the play farce or tragedy, there must be some spiritually significant idea, or it will hang lifeless. And this is what is lacking in *Henry V*.

What follows? We next find him writing three comedies, the three mature comedies as they are called: *As You Like It, Much Ado About Nothing, Twelfth Night.* Let us note one or two things about them.

The dominant characters are women, not men; that is one thing.

For another, in *As You Like It* and in *Much Ado About Nothing* it is almost as if he set out to write the plays in prose, as if he were sick of rhetoric, meant somehow to have an intimate, if a commonplace, medium to work in. But poets write poetry as ducks swim, and, at the first excuse, he drops back into it. And in *Twelfth Night,* the latest of the three, he has returned to his accustomed usage of both prose and verse, while his verse is still finding new freedom.

As usual, he borrows his stories, but his treatment of them is now really outrageous. In *As You Like It* it is a mere excuse for him to amuse himself and us in the Forest of Arden; and, when he must wind it up somehow, he does so with a perfunctoriness which makes the part of Jaques de Bois, introduced to that end, one of the laughing-stocks of the theatre. In *Much Ado* he lets it turn to ridicule; the end of the Claudio-Hero theme is cynically silly. In *Twelfth Night* he is a little more conscientious. Malvolio and his tormentors carry it away to the utter despite of Orsino and his high romance; but Viola holds her own. The value of *Much Ado* lies in the characters of Benedick and Beatrice and Dogberry, which are Shakespeare's arbitrary additions to the story. And in *As You Like It*, if Orlando and Rosalind are the story's protagonists (which Jaques and Touchstone certainly are not) yet the story itself may stand still while he develops them; and thankful we are that it should.

We need not insist upon the peculiarity of the three titles, though one is tempted to. *As You Like it, Much Ado About Nothing, What You Will!* As if they and the things they ostensibly stood for were bones thrown to the dogs of the audience, that wanted their plot and their ear-tickling jokes. Well, let them have it. Shakespeare meanwhile is doing what *he* will, and what he can do as no one else can, creating character, revealing character.

Then he finds his manly subject again in *Julius Caesar,* in that great theme of Rome and the old Roman world, which makes the matter of the English Histories seem parochial. How significant it must have been to any imaginative Englishmen of that age, with a new world of discovery, its chances and rivalries, its matter for thought and dreams opening up to him! Shakespeare was to return to Rome and the thought of Rome again and yet again; and he was never to return in thought – if he did in subject – to the narrower horizons. But note two things about *Julius Caesar.* We have no complaints of the inadequacy of his stage to the representing of the Senate or the battlefield of Philippi. On the contrary, he trusts in his fourth and fifth Acts to one of the oldest and simplest of Elizabethan conventions, the confronting upon the stage of two whole armies, symbolised by Generals, their standard-bearers and drummers. And whom does he choose as hero? Not Caesar himself, the triumphant, though doomed, man of action; but Brutus the philosopher, and the man, who for all his wisdom, invariably does the wrong thing. Brutus proves a not quite satisfactory dramatic hero. He is too unemotional, not impulsive enough; and Shakespeare, taking much of him ready made from Plutarch, never quite fathoms his stoicism. So first Cassius runs away with the play and then Mark Antony. When a character springs to life now Shakespeare is not going to refuse him his chance. Still, he resolutely comes back to the developing of Brutus. And his care is not for what his hero does, which is merely disastrous, but for what he *is*; this is the dramatic thing, and the essential thing.

> Thou seest the world Volumnius, how it goes;
> Our enemies have beat us to the pit . . .
>   Countrymen,
> My heart doth joy that yet in all my life,
> I found no man but he was true to me.
> I shall have glory by this losing day,
> More than Octavius and Mark Antony
> By this vile conquest shall attain unto.

If *Henry V* was the danger-point, *Julius Caesar* is the turning-point of Shakespeare's career.

Further, he is now rapidly bringing his verse to its dramatic perfection, is finally forming it into the supple and subtle instrument he needed. He had seldom, in trying to give it conversational currency, fallen into the pit — from which some of his contemporaries hardly emerged — of making it ten-syllabled prose. Rarely, rarely does one find such a line. Rhetoric was to be preferred to that, for rhetoric at least lifted drama to the higher emotional plane, except upon which it was hard to hold his audience in illusion. But he now relegates rhetoric to its proper dramatic place. Cassius is rhetorical by disposition; Antony because it suits his purpose. Shakespeare will bring his verse to a greater — and to a stranger — perfection yet. From now on, however, it is ever a more ductile and transparent medium, no bar either to the easy progress of a scene or to intimacy with a character.

But as the study of Brutus draws to an end do not the accents change a little? He is brooding on the issue of the coming battle.

>   O that a man might know
> The end of this day's business ere it come;
> But it sufficeth that the day will end
> And then the end is known.

Does not that echo to us a more familiar voice?

> If it be now, tis not to come; if it be not to come it will be now; if it be not now, yet it will come: the readiness is all; since no man has aught of what he leaves, what is't to leave betimes? Let be.

It is indeed the voice of Hamlet. And here was to be his next task. And here, not with *Henry V,* his crowning achievement.

It has been often enough remarked that Shakespeare had been making attempts at *Hamlet* all his playwright's life. We find a young euphuistic Hamlet in the first Act of Romeo, we find him in Richard II, and an impatient touch of him in Jaques. But now at last the daring, the inspired, the 'daemonic' partner in this dramatic firm once and fully and for all has his way with the amenable, politic play-provider. Yet, looking at it in the light of its success, do we realise what a breaking of bounds it was? By footrule criticism the thing has every fault. A play should be founded upon significant action; and this is about a man who never can make up his mind what to do, who, when he does do anything, does it by mistake. The story is interesting enough, and the device of the play within a play is a well-seasoned one. But the plot, as a plot, is worked out with scandalous ineptitude. At the play's most critical period the hero is absent from the stage for forty minutes, and the final tragedy is brought about by a precipitate and inartistic holocaust. And not only does Hamlet moralise about everything under the sun, but the rest of the characters — even the wretched Rosencrantz — follow his example upon the least excuse; and the whole thing is spun out to an intolerable length.

But the play was a success. Shakespeare the poet could have a good laugh at Shakespeare the popular playwright about that. And it has been the world's most consistently successful play ever since. And I think we can hear Shakespeare, the poet, saying, 'Yes, I know now what my theatre can do and what it can't. I know at least what *I* can do. Agincourt and its heroic swashbuckling — no! The stoic Brutus with his intellectual struggles? That was better, though it made hard going. But the passionate, suffering inner consciousness of man, his spiritual struggles and triumphs and defeats in his impact with an uncomprehending world — this may seem the most utterly unfit subject for such a crowded, noisy, vulgar place as the theatre; yet this is what I can make comprehensible, here is what I can do with my art.' And where now is that fine unstanding gentleman, Henry V? He is still at hand, and still commands our unreserved admiration.

But his name is Fortinbras, and he is often (though he shouldn't be) cut out of the play altogether.

Hamlet is the triumph of dramatic idea over dramatic action and of character over plot. Shakespeare – grant him the conventions of his stage, with the intimate value they give to the soliloquy and to the emotional privileges and demands of poetry – has now found the perfectly expressive character. The play in every circumstance, and Hamlet himself in every quality and defect, seem to answer the dramatist's need. He has found, moreover, perfect ease of expression. Verse, as he has now released it from its strictness, losing nothing of its rhythm, cannot, one would think, fall more aptly to the uses of dialogue than, say, in the scenes with Horatio and Marcellus, or to the direct expression of intimate emotion than in the soliloquy beginning

> O, what a rogue and peasant slave am I!
> Is it not monstrous that this player here . . .?

And we may note in passing that if in *Henry V* he was concerned with the disabilities of his stage, he now takes a chance of commenting on the art of acting, the more important matter of the two, by far. Further, that while the effect of the play within a play is greatly strengthened by letting the mimic play be of an older fashion (for thus there is less disturbance of the illusion created by the play of *Hamlet* which we are watching), he, in the very midst of his new-fashioned triumph, makes opportunity for a tribute to such men as were masters when he was but a prentice to his work. He has Hamlet speak of the play which was 'caviare to the general,' but of

> . . . an honest method, as wholesome as sweet, and by very much
> more handsome than fine.

How gracious a thing to do!

Shakespeare has written his masterpiece. What is to happen next? Will he try to repeat his success, or will he fall back upon amusing himself with pettier work? His restless genius lets him do neither. As becomes a great piece of dramatic art, *Hamlet* is too vital to be perfect; and he knows this, and it is evident that he submitted himself to criticism, his own, or other people's, or both. It was certainly much too long (I think it must always have been cut for ordinary performances). It does lack form; the knotting of its plot is cut rather than unravelled; and the other characters do many of them suffer from being written too much from Hamlet's point of view. Is this why in *Measure for Measure,* which probably was his next play,[3] we find Shakespeare confining himself within the bounds of a symmetrical story, done at normal length? But we find too, I think, that for all the beauty and ruthless wisdom of the play, he is not working happily. And in doing his duty by the plot, truth to character has to suffer violence at the end. Next comes *Othello.* Dr Bradley calls it the most masterly of the tragedies in the point of construction. Shakespeare is now obviously determined not to let himself be cramped by plot in the working out of character. There is no introspective hero to outbalance the play. He has another device – Iago's quite inhuman cunning – for letting us learn the inwardness of *Othello.* But he had, we see, to make a heroic effort to keep it a normal length. If he were not so successful one would take leave to call it an impudent effort; for as critic after critic has noted, and as one would think anybody of common sense among the audience could see for themselves, the compressions of the middle of the action make the whole plot impossible; there never *was* any moment when Desdemona could have been guilty of adultery with Cassio, and Othello must have known it. Shakespeare knew though, that common sense was the last faculty to be exercised in the theatre; or, to put it more advisedly, he knew that, once away from watches and clocks, we appreciate the relation of events rather by the intensity of the experiences which unite or divide them in our minds than by any arithmetical process. 'Short time' and 'long time' is less a definite dramatic device than a psychological commonplace – as most good dramatic devices are.

But he was now thinking of more than constructional compression and time-saving. He had opened up for himself a very

---

[3] Modern scholarship tends to date this play immediately after instead of before *Othello.* Moreover, *Troilus and Cressida* (and perhaps others) almost certainly came between *Hamlet* and the two plays in question.

complex artistic issue. Drama was to lie only formally in the external action, was to consist of the revelation of character and of the inevitable clashes between the natures of men. And besides, behind these there would be the struggle within a man's own nature; and the combatant powers there must be dramatised. (A living play is like life itself in this: each part of it is of the same nature as the whole, and partakes of the power of the whole.)

> Between the acting of a dreadful thing
> And the first motion, all the interim is
> Like a phantasma, or a hideous dream :
> The genius and the mortal instruments
> Are then in council ; and the state of man,
> Like to a little kingdom, suffers then
> The nature of an insurrection.

This is a recipe for tragedy. Brutus is speaking, but it might well be Macbeth. With Brutus the problem of dramatising this insurrection had been mainly avoided. In *Hamlet* it almost solved itself, for this was the very subject of the play; but one would not always happen upon so apt a story or so naturally histrionic a character. In *Othello* the problem is solved, as we have seen, by personifying the power of evil – and Shakespeare was a good Manichaean – in Iago. And in *Macbeth* he finds himself on the track of the same solution, with Lady Macbeth for an Iago. But he turns aside from the danger of self-imitation, somewhat to the truncating of her character.

Now, I think, the issue can be defined. These people of his imagining had to be made to show us their innermost selves, and to show us things in themselves of which they were not themselves wholly conscious. Further, the physical and moral atmosphere in which they move, and its effect on them, will be of importance. All this apart from the telling of the story and the outward contest! Yet in this complex task he can look for no help worth speaking of but from interpretative acting. To what else could he look? Scenery, in the illusionary sense, he had none. Pageantry may be very well on occasion, but it is apt to leave your drama precisely where it found it. He had the spoken word. But he could not let his characters dissipate the audience's interest in themselves with long descriptions

of outward things. While, if for intimate revelation the soliloquy
has been till now, and must always be, a great resource, too
many soliloquies do undoubtedly relax the tension and weaken
the structure of a play. And I think we may notice that from
Othello onwards they are either shorter or more sparingly used.
No; he has to fall back on dialogue, and on a fair proportion of
short-range hard-hitting dialogue, if his characters are to seem
to hold each other's attention or are to hold the audience's
upon these not very simple questions. He has done with
passages of rock-like rhetoric, which so obviously soar over the
person they are addressed to for a landing in the back of the
gallery (though Shakespeare the popular playwright must still
be allowed one or two, that a scene may be rounded off in the
recognised way). In fine, then, the physical conditions of his
theatre, combined with the needs of his art as he now perceives
them, drive him to depend for story-telling, character-building,
and scene-painting upon what can be made of the art of the
actor alone. Moreover – here is the point – for brevity's sake
and for the sake of the tenseness, by which alone an audience
can be held in the bonds of illusion, he must find some formula
of dramatic speech into which these three things can be
wrought, all three together.

It is in *Macbeth* that he seems most directly to face this
problem; how he solves it remains his secret. Maeterlinck, in a
preface to his own translation of the play,[4] gives a masterly
analysis of the effect created. I wish I could quote it at length.
But this is his summing up :

> A sa suface flotte le dialogue nécessaire à l'action. Il semble le
> seul qu'entendent les oreilles; mais en réalité c'est l'autre parole
> qu'écoute notre instinct, notre sensibilité inconsciente, notre âme
> si l'on veut; et si les mots extérieurs nous atteignent plus pro-
> fondément qu'en nul autre poète, c'est qu'une plus grande foule
> de puissances cachées les supporte.[5]

---

[4] Paris, 1910.

[5] 'On the surface floats the dialogue necessary for the action. It seems the
only one that our ears hear; but actually it is another speech that is heard by
our instinct, our unconscious sensibility, our soul if you will; and if the
external words affect us more profoundly than those of any other poet, it is
because a great crowd of hidden powers support them.'

And he remarks that throughout the play we find practically no 'expressions mortes' [dead expressions].

But that is not to explain, of course, how lines are written which – in their place – will have the magic of

> Light thickens,
> And the crow makes wing to the rooky wood.

or the power – though it seems, and is, a line a child might write – of

> It will have blood: they say blood will have blood.

Or that can give the effect – really one cannot remove this from its place – of Macduff's.

> He has no children.

There is, finally, no explaining the marvel of the sleep-walking scene (if only actors would not try to make it more of a marvel and so make it less!), in which Lady Macbeth speaks but sixteen sentences, of which the most distinctive are merely such simplicities as

> Hell is murky.

as

> The Thane of Fife had a wife; where is she now?

as

> All the perfumes of Arabia will not sweeten this little hand.

('Little' hand! Mark its placing in the sentence and its significance. One may divine touches like that.)

Here then is a secret that Shakespeare mastered and never lost, and that no one else has ever found. It is during the period of his work which covers *Macbeth, King Lear* and *Antony and Cleopatra,* that he wields the magic of it most potently. But the spell is not fully operative – this we must always remember – unless we are within the charmed circle of the play itself. And when Bradley says, and surely says rightly, that Lear's last speech –

And my poor fool is hang'd! No, no; no life!
Why should a dog, a horse, a rat, have life,
And thou no breath at all? Thou'lt come no more,
Never, never, never, never, never!
Pray you, undo this button; thank you, sir,
Do you see this? Look on her, look, her lips,
Look there, look there!

— leaves us upon the topmost pinnacles of poetry, people who cannot transport themselves into the magic world of the living play must wonder what on earth he means.

Whatever *is* there in Antony's

I am dying, Egypt, dying; only
I here importune death a while, until
Of many thousand kisses the poor last
I lay upon thy lips.

Or — as she holds the aspic to her — in Cleopatra's failing

Peace, peace!
Dost thou not see my baby at my breast,
That sucks the nurse asleep?

And, returning to *Macbeth*, can we even account for the full effect of such passages as the familiar

I have liv'd long enough : my way of life
Is fall'n into the sear, the yellow leaf . . .

or

To-morrow and to-morrow and to-morrow . . .

Shakespeare keeps his secret.

Macbeth is the shortest of the tragedies : even could we restore the probable mutilations I expect it would still be the shortest. It is the most concentrated, the most stripped and stark. In spite of all the circumstances of its form, it comes, as has been said, the nearest to Greek tragedy. A last look at it gives us the figures of Macbeth and his wife carved, monumental and aloof, as if Sophocles had been at them. Was it a success? It was given one or more Court performances. James I, with all his faults, had a taste for good drama; or if he only pretended to one, it would, for me, be a pardonable piece of snobbery. Still, it is significant that the folio editors found nothing but a text which Middleton had been called in to enliven with song and dance.

But now note that for his next task our reckless genius flings off to the very opposite extreme.[6] In *King Lear* he provides himself with a doubled plot, whose working out would leave him with a longer play than Hamlet; and from this mischance he saves himself only by the most heroic measures. Moreover, in Lear himself he finds a character who runs away with him as no other has done yet. It is the play of his widest outlook. In *Julius Caesar* he thought he was taking a world view. But he stood at Plutarch's side and perhaps did not understand all he saw. This is his own vision; and from this mountain top what we should now call his social conscience searches widest. Anatole France, speaking of great men, has another word for it.

La pitié, voyez-vous, M. le Professeur, c'est le fond même du génie.[7]

And if Shakespeare had looked into his new edition of the Bible he would have found in a pertinent passage yet another word freshly restored there, the word 'charity.' By this test, here is his greatest play.

How does he marshal his resources?

The play starts off disciplined and conventional, promising to be as 'Greek' as *Macbeth* has been. But in the development of Lear himself — and to this for a time everything gives way and everything contributes — Shakespeare soon breaks all bounds. He rallies every stage device he can think of: even the now old-fashioned figure of the Fool is turned to account — and to what account! But above all, his theme requires that he shall relate Lear to the crude world we live in, and to the rigours

---

[6] I am, it seems, in error in placing *Macbeth* before *King Lear*. I must accept, to that extent, the vitiation of my argument. (Granville-Barker's note, 1932)

[7] 'Pity, you see Professor, is the very foundation of genius.' *Propos d'Anatole France* (*Les Matinées de la villa Saïd*), recueillis par Paul Gsell, Paris: Grasset, 1921, p. 146.

of that world as it may fall on rich and poor alike – as it must
fall, crushingly for his purpose, upon the proud old tyrant himself. He needs that storm, as he needed the mob in *Caesar,* the
ghost in *Hamlet,* or the personified evil of Iago. How does he
create it? We are far from the Chorus' apologetics of *Henry V*
for what the stage could *not* provide. We are far even from the
technique of *Julius Caesar,* where Cicero, Cassius, and Casca
are set to describe at length, though little to the advancement
of the play, the tempest that heralded the great murder. Shakespeare is for bolder methods now. He turns one character,
Edgar, in his disguise as a wandering, naked, half-witted
beggar, into a veritable piece of scene-painting of the barren,
inhospitable heath. And for the storm itself, he shows it us in
its full play as a reflection of that greater storm which rages in
the mind of Lear – of anger, terror, pity, remorse – lightening
and darkening it as a storm does the sky, and finally blasting it
altogether. For *that* storm, as Shakespeare knows now, is the
really dramatic thing; and it is the only thing that his art can
directly and satisfactorily present. To say no more of it than this,
here is a marvellous piece of stagecraft, the finest and most
significant single thing he ever did – and some of the best
critics have decided that in itself it makes the play impossible
for the stage!

At which stumbling-block of a paradox we may end this
journey. We need not glance on towards *Antony and Cleopatra,*
which is in some ways the most perfect, and altogether, I think,
the most finely spacious piece of play-making he ever did; nor
to *Coriolanus*, where he managed at last to make his 'man of
action' dramatically effective; nor to the latest romances, fruits
of a well-earned and tolerant repose.

But is *King Lear* unfitted for the stage and so a failure? We
cannot turn the question by contemning the theatre itself. A
play written to be acted, which cannot be effectively acted, is a
failure. What should we say of a symphony which no orchestra
could play? And the answer to this question will, as I contend,
involve, though with a difference, all these greater plays that
we have been considering. The question will indeed become:
did Shakespeare, when with *Henry V* he came to the end of all
he could find to his purpose in the technique of the drama

as his contemporaries and masters understood it, when, passing over that bridge which is *Julius Caesar,* he found in the working out of *Hamlet* the technique best suited to his genius, did he then and thereafter take the wrong road? One had better not be too ready with a straight Yes or No. Frankly, I am for Shakespeare the playwright and No. It is a hard road, but not a blind one; it leads us ahead. If you are for Shakespeare the playwright, what other answer can there be? But much critical authority – though it will not quite say Yes – is still apt to imply it. Through all the important appreciation of his greater work there flows an undercurrent of something very like resentment that he should have been so ill-advised, so inconsiderate as to write it for the theatre at all. And if some of those ingenious contrivers on his behalf of 'short time' and 'long time' could bring that useful system into a sort of retrospective operation in real life that would abolish the three hundred odd years which separates them from him, could they meet him for a talk during that crisis in his career, happen on him, for instance, just when he was discerning what the working out of the theme of *Hamlet* was to involve, I fancy they would advise him in all friendliness that the subject really was not suitable for a play. Had he asked in return what form, then, he had better cast it in (and it would be a fair question): well, there is the Platonic dialogue; there is the example of Milton turning deliberately from drama to the epic; and Goethe could be held up to him as an awful warning. Beethoven was the luckier man. He could write symphonies in which to enshrine such tremendous emotions; from him descend the great dramatic poets we choose rather to listen to to-day, and music is their language. To which Shakespeare might answer that his Elizabethans felt the need and responded to the art of personal expression more than we do, whose minds are full of science and machinery and of all sorts of things, actual and speculative, that cannot be reduced to terms of human emotion. 'Though can they not be?' he might add, 'and must they not be at any rate brought within the range of it, if you are really to comprehend them?' He might even be able to refer to a remark which that sympathetic Frenchman, Monsieur André Maurois, has let fall lately in a current book of his – in no way about the theatre, and truly it is written in particular about the French – concerning the universal 'besoin de mimer.'[8] Monsieur Maurois sees this need of physical expression as the sign of a well-balanced being. A mind isolated from the body, which should be its reflection and its picturing, will be no more effective, he says, than a bird trying to fly in the ether instead of in the air. And after all, Shakespeare might argue, the final test to which everything in the world, great or small, good or evil, must be brought is its effect upon man himself; not upon your economic man, your democratic man, your man-in-the-street, nor any other of the abstractions which Governments and able editors are now concerned with, but upon that strange mixture of thought, appetite and immortal soul – 'a poor forked animal he may be, but I make my king own to brotherhood with him. And the claim of this drama of mine,' he would say, 'as I have now evolved it, is to bring you into immediate and intimate contact with that man as he essentially *is,* in an *ever present tense.* What other art can do this as mine can?'

That is a fine claim, no doubt; but the practical question remains whether, considering the limits of time and all the other limits and imperfections of the theatre itself, considering its motley mixture of an audience of poor forked animals and kings, considering not least the limitations and imperfections of the actors themselves – does the dramatist seriously expect a company of these actors, decked in borrowed clothes and borrowed passions, strutting the bare boards for an hour or so, to compass these tasks he had set them?

To which Mr Shakespeare, for all his famed gentleness, might reply rather tartly: 'My dear sir, I was an actor myself. I may not have been a very good one; that was partly because I could not give my whole mind to it, for the writing of even such a trifle as *The Merry Wives of Windsor* takes it out of a man. But I know a good deal more of the possibilities of the art of acting than you do; and am I likely to have been so inconsiderate and so foolish as to risk the success of any play by setting its actors tasks that they could *not* perform?'

---

[8] 'need to mimic' (in the sense of expressing emotional states by physical gestures). I have been unable to locate the source.

Excellent repartee; but it still does not settle the question. It is absurd to suppose that such a restless and daring genius would check himself in full career to ask whether Burbage and his fellows could do well with this and that sort of scene or not. Without doubt Shakespeare imagined effects, which never were fully achieved in his theatre. But there is a great gulf fixed between this admission and saying that he imagined effects that never *could* be achieved, saying, in fact, that he ceased altogether to write in the terms of the art he had mastered. Genius is often a destructive force, and the question is a fair one, and we may press it: did Shakespeare in his greatest work, trying to enlarge, only shatter his medium? Yet before we credit this last accusation, think of the masters of other arts – of music especially – whose most mature work was received at best with the respect to which earlier success had entitled them, but with the protest that really these Ninth Symphonies and these music dramas were but negations of music. Yet what difficulty do we find in appreciating them now?

Posterity's answer, as given to the great revolutionary masters of music, has been, by one chance and another denied to Shakespeare; for these greater plays have never yet been put to full theatrical proof. To begin with, the theatre for which he wrote was itself undergoing one revolutionary change even before he ceased writing for it; it was shifting from outdoors in. To compare the effect of this upon his plays to the bringing of the *Agamemnon* into the back drawing-room would be an exaggeration, but with a strong spice of truth in it. Then came suppression of the theatres; tradition was broken, its thread lost, and more was lost than this. Contemporary evidence points to it, even if study of Restoration drama did not. We must always question very closely the testimony of people who mourn the 'good old times,' especially the good old times of the drama. No performances are better than those of our earliest recollection; and I suppose it follows that the best of all must be those we never saw. (These, however, are the actor's means of immortality; so let us not grudge them to him.) But when the speakers in the dialogue *Historia Histrionica* in 1699, looking back sixty years, refer to the actors of the King's Company, which was Shakespeare's, as having been 'grave and sober men, living in reputation,' it is likely to be the truth; for there is confirmation of it. Heminge and Condell were two of them. Does not the introduction to the first folio reflect as much gravity and sobriety as you like? Consider, too, that for fifty years here was a guild (that best describes it) of great renown, with many privileges, for long attached to the Court. No women were admitted; and this, at the time (and even now perhaps) would make for its greater gravity. Its younger recruits were the boy apprentices, thoroughly and severely trained from their childhood. It was a body made to perpetuate tradition. This first chance to come abreast with the greater Shakespeare passed. It passed with the deaths of Shakespeare and Burbage. The theatre had its daily bread to earn and fashion to follow. A re-creative interpretative genius would have been needed. And with the Puritan revolution it vanished. Then followed the demoralisation of the Restoration period. Betterton did much to rescue the theatre, but he developed a more Augustan tradition, which dominated the eighteenth and much of the nineteenth century. This was a time, too, of the mutilation of texts in the theatre, though scholars were restoring them in the study; also of Shakespeare by flashes of lightning, those flashes of lightning that are apt to leave us in deeper darkness between times. Nineteenth-century scholarship suffered from a surfeit of Shakespeare as philosopher, Shakespeare as mystic, as cryptogrammatic historian, as this and that, and as somebody else altogether. And the nineteenth-century theatre suffered from the nineteenth century; it was commercialised. Till at last it has seemed but common sense to return to Shakespeare as playwright, and even, for a fresh start, to Shakespeare as Elizabethan playwright. Upon which basis we have within these last five-and-twenty years largely relaid the foundations of our study of him. For this latter-day pioneering we have to thank scholars and men of the theatre both, men of diverse, not to say antagonistic, minds, methods, and standpoints. Mr William Poel, with a fine fanaticism, set himself to show us the Elizabethan stage as it was. Dr Pollard put us on the track of prompt-books. Dr Chambers, Sir Israel Gollancz (if in his presence I may name him), Mr Lawrence, Mr Dover Wilson — we are in debt to many. And one I will more particularly name; William

Archer, whose death five months ago was a bitter blow to his friends and a heavy loss to the causes he loved and served. He loved the theatre of the past – though at times he might dissemble his love – not less because he felt the theatre of the present needed his watchful praise and criticism more. To this present question he brought industry and knowledge, and to his writings on it a generosity of judgement, which was only to be chilled by his intolerance of slovenliness and humbug; in fact, to this, as to all his work, he brought the standards by which he lived, of constancy and truth.

We have set ourselves, then, for a fresh start, to see Shakespeare the playwright as his contemporaries – as my old playgoer of 1635, whom I fear I have been forgetting, whom I will now finally forget – saw him. But even so we must not narrow our view. More is involved than the mere staging of his plays, than the question whether they must be acted in a reproduction of the Globe Theatre or may be decked out in all the latest trimmings. We know well enough what the Elizabethan stage was like. We do not know fully all the effects that could be gained on it, for only experiment will show us. Such experimenting, therefore, will always be valuable. But surely this principle can be agreed upon; that, whether or no one can ever successfully place a work of art in surroundings for which it was not intended, at least one must not submit it to conditions which are positively antagonistic to its technique and its spirit. Such an agreement involves, in practice, for the staging of Shakespeare – first, from the audience, as much historical sense as they can cultivate without it choking the spring of their spontaneous enjoyment; next, that the producer distinguish between the essentials and the incidentals of the play's art. Many even of its essentials may be closely knit to the Elizabethan stage of its origin. But whether it is to be played upon a platform or behind footlights, whether with curtains or scenery for a background (and scenery which is more than a background sins even against its own nature) this at least is clear, if my contention of to-day be allowed: Shakespeare's progress in his art involved an ever greater reliance upon that other art which *is* irrevocably wedded to the playwright's – the art of interpretative acting.

And it is in this aspect – of the demands which his greatest work makes upon acting according to the privilege which the technique he evolved bestows upon it – that his art has not yet, I think, been either very fruitfully studied or illustrated. Nor, for the historical reasons I have given, do I see how it well could have been. Nor is the path to its studying very easy even now. There are gleams of light along it, but only gleams. From the scholar's side we had, a generation ago, Moulton's *Shakespeare as a Dramatic Artist*; the work of a powerful mind, a little apt in the excess of its power to break its subject in pieces and remould it as stern logic requires, but a book nevertheless which does elucidate some of the fundamental things in which Shakespeare's art abides. When Dr Bradley's masterly *Shakespearean Tragedy* was given us – this was a bright gleam, though it still surprised some people a little to find an Oxford professor treating not only poetry as poetry, but plays as plays. Nowadays, however, Sir Arthur Quiller-Couch takes lucky Cambridge men for delightful picnics (may one so call them?) in the sunny meads of literature, dramatic and other. And we even find him publicly confessing that he stage-managed a performance of *The Merchant of Venice* a few years ago and learned a lot about the play in the process. And if this is the first the Chancellor of that dignified University hears of such a shameful fact, I hope that he hears it unmoved.[9]

There is always a danger, however, that the scholar, approaching a play from its histrionic standpoint, may trip himself up over some simple snag. This is unfortunate and unfair; for after all it is a very proper way of approach. But the drama is an old art; it cannot be wholly reduced to the terms of the printed page. To printer and publisher and editor it bows with gratitude. Where would Shakespeare be to-day without them? Much of its practice, however, particularly on its histrionic side, can only be handed down from master to pupil in the traditional way, as other arts and mysteries are. But in this present case and at the present time the artists fail us too, I fear. Their individual excellence is not in question, but that opportunity for

---

[9] The late Lord Balfour was in the chair. (Granville-Barker's note) Balfour died in 1930.

constant collaboration which is the theatre's peculiar need, by which tradition is formed and preserved. We have no care for the traditions of our theatre.[10] Within my own day one school of Shakespearean acting has perished; it was not a very good one, but it had its own virtues. The present attempts at a new one are being made under conditions that cannot at any rate make it fit for the task we are discussing now. I would not say one word in discouragement of the efforts of the hard-worked young men and women who gallantly fly the flag and have the trumpet blown for them at Stratford-on-Avon and the Old Vic, and elsewhere. Theirs is a very necessary task. But it is conditioned by the fact that they must be constantly providing a three-hours' entertainment for their audience. To that overriding necessity everything else must give way. Now there are many plays – plays of Shakespeare's too – that fulfil such conditions very well. Act them, if not a little better, then a little worse, and no great harm is done. But the five great tragedies do not come into that category. Viewed as an evening's entertainment *King Lear is* a foredoomed failure, even as Beethoven's great Mass and Bach's Matthew Passion would be. For it comes, as they come, into another category of art altogether; it is not the art that by perfect and pretty performance will charm and soothe us, but that which, in the classic phrase, purges by pity and terror. We don't expect to enjoy the Mass as we do *The Mikado,* or even as we may enjoy a Mozart sonata. There is as much enjoyment of the common sort in *King Lear* as there is in a shattering spiritual experience of our own; though we may come to look back on both with gratitude for the wisdom they have brought us. Incidentally, the due interpretation of such art will purge the interpreters with mental and emotional and

---

[10] Something is, I believe, being done to preserve the beauty of English speech; gramophone records of it are now kept at the British Museum. How like the time! Have they a record, I wonder, of the most beautiful piece of speaking I ever heard, Sir Johnston Forbes Robertson's 'Buckingham's Farewell' in *Henry VIII*? I have been waiting for thirty years and more to hear it again. But he has never played the part again, has never had the chance. Were we so rich in such talent that we could afford to let it be spent at large? And we are to tell our students of to-day that they can hear it on the gramophone! It is not by such creaking methods that artistic tradition is handed on. (Granville-Barker's note) Forbes-Robertson played Buckingham in Irving's revival at the Lyceum in 1892.

physical exhaustion too. It demands from them an extraordinary self-devotion. Its greatest effects may be within their reach, but will always be a little beyond their grasp. Actors and singers are brought to the point where they forget themselves and we forget them. And beyond that boundary – it may happen to some of us a dozen times in a lifetime to cross it – we are for a crowning moment or so in a realm of absolute music and of a drama that Shakespeare's genius will seem to have released from all bonds. I say that we must not look for perfect performances of such plays, for there is nothing so finite as perfection about them. They have not the beauty of form and clarity of expression which distinguish Racine and his great Greek exemplars. But, in virtue of a strange dynamic force that resides in them, they seem to surpass such perfection and to take on something of the quality of life itself. And they do this the more fitly, surely, in that they demand to be interpreted, less conventionally, in terms of life itself, through this medium of living men and women. Therefore, while we arrive at no perfection in their performance, there need be practically no limit to, nor any monotony in the inspiration actors can draw from them. And their essential technique is likely to lie in the fruitfulness and variety of the means by which the significance of human relations – of men towards each other, of man to the invisible – is revealed. A later theatre has made for us an illusion by which we see men as beings of another world. But Shakespeare worked for an intimacy which should break the boundaries between mimic and real, and identify actor and audience upon the plane of his poetic vision. Is there another art in which the world of the imagination can be made so real to us and the immaterial so actual, in which, not to speak it profanely, the word can be made flesh, as in these few boldest flights of his genius?

I do not pretend that I have fathomed Shakespeare's secret; my contention is that it has not been fathomed yet, and that it cannot be given to the world by such means as we have now at hand. The scholar, at best, will be in the case of a man reading the score of a symphony, humming the themes. He may study and re-study a play, and ever find something new. I have seen and read *Julius Caesar* times enough, and now at the moment

I am flattering myself with the discovery – though doubtless it is *not* a new one – that the decried last Act is a masterpiece. Again, who will not confess with me that at any performance some quite unsuspected effect (unsuspected often by the interpreters themselves) may suddenly glow into life before him? For instances: the fullness of tragic irony that resides in the very meeting of the jovial sensualist Gloucester, deprived of his eyes, with Lear, the man of intellectual pride, robbed of his wits; the edge given to the tragedy in Othello, when he and Desdemona, on the brink of the abyss, must yet concern themselves with entertaining the Venetian envoy to dinner. These are little things; but as we saw, the great plan of the plays apart, it is the wealth of such touches, many of which can hardly be expressed in other terms than the art's own, that endow them with their abundant life.

Can the full virtue of any art be enjoyed except in its own terms? This is the crucial question. To transport Shakespeare from the world of the theatre into a vacuum of scholarship is folly. Must we say (I will not admit it) that in the theatre scholarship cannot find a place? But the conditions under which the theatre works to-day – and always has worked in England – are no more compatible with the stricter obligations of scholarship than is any other form of journalism. The theatre to-day does much that is effective, even as many journalists write exceedingly well. But if the higher tasks of literature had all to be essayed with the printer's devil as call-boy at the door, heaven help us!

So here is a high task and a hard task, and a task, as I contend, never fully attempted yet. For Shakespeare *did* in these greater imaginings break through the boundaries of the material theatre he knew, and none that we have yet known has been able to compass them. Can such a theatre be brought to being? How can we say till we have tried? But as he never ceased to be the practical playwright and man of the theatre the chances are, perhaps, that it can. Only, however, I believe, by providing for some continuance of that guild of grave and sober men of reputation to whom the work was first a gift. A gift too great for them, perhaps; is it still too great a one for us? Or can we, after three centuries, amid the never-ceasing chatter of tribute to Shakespeare as the marvel of our race, also contrive to make his art at its noblest a living thing?

No need to discuss here how such a guild could be formed. There are fifty ways of doing it if we had the will. But a first clause in its charter would need to secure the privilege which all good scholars claim – for its members would be scholars in their kind – that the work should be done for its own sake. It would involve hard discipline, in the retracing and re-treading of the road upon which Shakespeare as playwright passed and beckoned. The foundations of poetic drama, this most national of our arts, would need to be retrodden firm. It is not, even in its genesis, the art of slinging fine blank-verse lines together upon a printed page, but – and here the first thing to restore – the art of speech made eloquent by rhythm and memorable by harmony of sense and sound. For here was Shakespeare's first strength; from this he advanced. And if we cared to follow him faithfully for the hard length of his pilgrimage, scholars of the printed page side by side with scholars of the spoken word, it might be that we could enter into and enjoy that still mysterious country of his highest art. An inheritance, one would suppose, well worth the effort and the journey!

'From Henry V to Hamlet,'
in *Aspects of Shakespeare, Being British Academy Lectures [1923–1931]*, ed. J. W. Mackail, Oxford: The Clarenden Press, 1933, pp. 49–83.

A revised edition of the British Academy Annual Shakespeare Lecture on May 13, 1925, published in *Proceedings of the British Academy*, XI, 1924–1925, London: Humphrey Milford for Oxford University Press, 1926, pp. 283–309.